Old Nantasket

THE NANCY

The Famous Stranded Schooner *Nancy* on February 20, 1927, when it was driven ashore on Nantasket Beach after delivering her cargo of coal in Boston. She started back, light, for Norfolk, Va. when storm warnings were posted. Her captain decided to drop anchor at the entrance of Boston Harbor and ride out the storm. A sixty mile an hour gale snapped the anchor chains and the big ship was driven high up on the beach. She was finally blown apart and burned. Her keel lies buried in the beach sand. *(Courtesy Stradi Karas)*

Old Nantasket

By

DR. WILLIAM M. BERGAN

Fort Revere Park & Preservation Society
in partnership with Times Square Books
Hull, Massachusetts

TO MY WIFE

MARION

AND OUR FOUR DAUGHTERS

TABLE OF CONTENTS

FOREWORD

Here, in the robust language and inimitable style of the author, is an authentic picture of a period in the history of Nantasket. It was a day in which the old Anglo-Saxon words were in common parlance. Bergan knows them all and uses some of them. How else the truth? How else write a living document about the strange vitality of those amazing times?

William M. Bergan, 78, was a member of the old "Ring" where he received his political schooling. He is a former Chairman of the Board of Selectmen and was an active participant in the affairs about which he writes.

"While you live, tell truth, and shame the devil!"

Mason A. Foley
March, 1968

Old Nantasket

I

THE PILGRIMS – PLYMOUTH COUNTY

In a corner of famed Plymouth County, where the Pilgrims landed and our country began, rests the little town of Hull, Massachusetts, almost surrounded by "the shining big sea water." It was cleared and settled by the Pilgrims, with the authority of the Mayflower Compact, and watched over by the spiritual advisor of the Pilgrims, Elder William Brewster.

Before landing at Plymouth, while the ship was still at anchor, the forty-one men met in the cabin of the *Mayflower*, drew up and signed an agreement promising, "In the presence of God and one another all due submission and obedience" as they might find necessary. This document is known in history as "The Mayflower Compact." The forty-one signers are known as "The Pilgrim Fathers."

After the passing of the first winter and spring, the *Mayflower*, anchored in the bay, prepared to set sail. Although half of their original number lay in the little burial ground, not one of the Pilgrims expressed a wish to return to England.

Any structure that has grown as great as our country has, and has not toppled, must have been built on an extremely strong foundation.

The little acorn had to have all the mighty oak was made of. All that was America was here then. All that is America is here now.

Who am I, the son of Irish immigrants, to evaluate the grandeur of the Pilgrim? When I see what they were made of it is honor enough for me to be born where our country was born and to have lived my life in this "clearance in the forest" made by the Pilgrim Fathers.

For the next 200 years our country was in the formative state. Measured by present-day standards of progress, there

13

was none. They and their descendants, plain, sincere folk, followed the golden rule to the letter. Helpfulness to one another was their natural choice. It was also necessary to their survival. They had the double incentive of wanting to do what they had to do anyway. Helpfulness to one another was the little acorn. The mighty oak was to follow.

The British Empire of that time was, by far, the most powerful nation on earth. "The sun never set on British soil," and "Britannia ruled the waves." The fabric that was woven together by living the golden rule for 200 years was strong enough to make Lord Cornwallis fork over his sword at Yorktown, and it polished off the British again in the War of 1812.

It seems that starting with my boyhood, here in the small town of Hull, in the 1890's and for the next half century, tracing out my own lifetime may best highlight the trends in our changing times.

We lived, as I can barely remember, in an old leaky five-room house; a water pump in the sink connected to the well outside; the only heat, a black, iron kitchen stove, instead of the open fireplace; kerosene lamps for tallow candles; and, of course, the little house out back. You can have all your rankings about privy, rest room, powder room and comfort station, but when I was a boy it was a shithouse. That's what it was called then by young and old alike, and when we recall the stench, the maggots and the green flies, there could be no question, either then or now, but that shithouse was its proper name. No lavender toilet tissue then. You just grabbed a handful of leaves on the way out.

My father stocked our cellar with provisions for the winter, including three barrels of cider – not the sweet kind sold in supermarkets – but the well-fermented kind. Maximum intoxication was attained in the third glass. I remember peeking down cellar and seeing him and some of his cronies loaded to the gills. We boys got that way a few times, too.

The house was banked around with seaweed and, like other farm families in the area, when the cold weather came we crawled in and pulled the hole in after us. Our mode of living was not much different from the Pilgrims.

One winter evening, while my mother was polishing the kitchen stove, a knock was heard at the door. A man entered and in a thick Irish brogue said that he and my father were old cronies in Ireland years ago, and that the first thing he wanted to do when he came to this country, was to look him up. My mother got the teapot out. She told him my father was not home. They talked for a while. He said he would come again. As he was leaving, the door half open, he turned and told my mother that my father was as fine an Irishman as ever straddled a pot.

In 1896, I was sent to a first grade one-room school just over the town line in Cohasset. It was heated by a pot-belly, wood burning stove. We had to bring in the wood, carry out the ashes and sweep the floor. The amount of work each did depended on his behavior. Our teacher was a very severe elderly lady. If a boy did something wrong she would drag him up in front of the class, take down his pants and smash his bare ass eight or ten times with a rough board. I never saw anyone go back for a second helping. Seeing the behavior of today's children, that's a custom that should never have been dropped.

The privy out back had four holes on the boys' side and four on the girls'. One morning the teacher went out to the girls' side. When she came back she flew into such a damn fit of rage that George Washington's picture fell off the wall. She emptied the classroom and sent everybody home. One of the boys had sneaked in back of the privy and tickled her behind with a goldenrod. The school was closed for two days until she found out who had done it. The poor boy never came back. His parents knew what would happen to him, so they sent him to another school.

I went from there to a local grammar school. One day, while in the fourth grade, after school was dismissed I was on my way home when I forgot my books and went back to what I thought was an empty classroom. When I went in the janitor had his hand up under the teacher's dress. My embarrassment was somewhat relieved when they explained that he was only fixing her garter. Like the smart fish I kept my mouth shut. I got the only "A" I ever got on a report card in my life and I got it for the rest of the term. Had I peeked into a few more rooms, I might have been principal of the school.

In the fifth grade the teacher in the classroom asked little Johnny to stand up and say something that rhymed. He said:

"There was a pretty winsome lass
Who stood in the water up to her knees"

The teacher said, "That doesn't rhyme." He said, "It will when the tide comes in."

Our home is located by a beautiful sandy beach. Hundreds of thousands come to bathe here each summer. They open the trunks of their cars and go to the beach with mattresses, pillows, blankets, tents, beach chairs, umbrellas, life preservers and dozens of other gadgets. If they brought a couple of camels along they would resemble the Arabs of Old. When we were boys we went swimming down the river. Anyone who had a bathing suit was a sissy. The fact that none of us were sissies was just another indication of our changing times.

There are more pills, drugs and medicines in the bathroom cabinet of a modern home than there were in the old-time drugstore. The only damn thing we ever saw was a bottle of castor oil.

While we may be amused by the youth of today who needs a car to take him to the bathroom, we must be careful to make judicial use of our good fortune and enjoy these new advantages in a manner that will not provoke the envy of other lands, nor have their softening influence rub off on our own national character.

After the sixth grade, summer vacation came and my early training in politics started with my first job as caddy at the nearby Cohasset Golf Club. We were paid twenty-five cents for the lost balls that we found. I had a good start. I sold them four balls for one dollar. The man I caddied for the day before reported four balls missing from his golf bag. A short investigation was held and I was fired because I found them before they got lost. I should have thrown them against the stone wall a few times and dented them up. It showed me that if you're going to steal you had better cover up your tracks.

In our high-school German class the teacher, a pretty young lady, asked us to prepare a statement in German for our next day's lesson. So I got hold of an old German friend of mine. He sat up all night teaching me to say and write, "I Love You Dear Teacher, I Really Do." As she was going through the papers that were turned in she ran across mine. She stood up and yelled, "Bergan go out of the room." Then, as I was going out the door, she said. "Get back in your seat." I learned right then that if you say something nice to a lady, though she may resent it at first, she will always like you for it.

In grammar school I failed to graduate with my class and had to go back another year. The same thing happened in high school. It happened again in Dental School, I had to go back another year for my degree. My flair for the foolish and my spotty academic background accounts for the clumsy way this thing is written.

II

THE BIG HOTEL

This town was called Nantascot by the Wampanoag Indians. In 1644, the name was changed to Hull from the seaport town of Hull on the Humber, in Yorkshire, England. The spelling has varied since those early days and the place has come to be known far and wide as Nantasket and Hull is not very well-known. We must use the official name in reference to its government and political machine but we will also use the name Nantasket that has become so famous in the world outside.

From the early 1880's to just before World War I was the era of the big hotel, the celebrity, rampant gambling and machine government. All this took place before the advent of the automobile. The Rockland House, the Atlantic House, the Nantasket Hotel, the Villa Napoli, the Pacific House and the Pemberton Hotel were the largest and better-known hotels in the Nantasket area.

The Rockland House, situated on the hill back of Paragon Park, was the largest summer hotel in the United States. Established in 1854 by Colonel Nehemiah Ripley, the house was enlarged at various times from its original capacity of thirty rooms to 360. The building was four stories high and about 320 feet long. The property has been conducted at different periods by famous hotel men, the number including the late Amos Whipple. The hotel was later the property of Patrick Bowen, ex-Alderman and proprietor of the New Marlboro Hotel in Boston.

While I was studying at Tufts College Dental School, a young man named Joseph Mulhern, who later became a noted doctor in Worcester, Massachusetts, hospitals, was then

ROCKLAND HOUSE, 1879

a student in Tufts Medical School in the same building. During the summer vacation he was a bellboy at the Rockland House. The way I had to scratch and save to squeeze by in school made a place like the Rockland House off limits to me. He brought me in and showed me around. The place was empty on the morning that he first took me through, but I was stunned and amazed at the huge ballroom, the dazzling chandeliers, the beautiful curtains and draperies, the banquet tables and chairs around the rim of the hall, the dance area in the center and the low stage at the far end with the orchestra enclosure off to one side. He showed me two large gambling rooms with elaborate roulette wheels, the little stalls around the wheels where the players' money was kept and the rake that pushed the money around where it should go. He showed me the dice tables and how they operated, the poker tables with a square marked on them in front of each player where his money was kept and a circle toward the center of the table where his ante should be, black jack tables and other gambling paraphernalia that I didn't understand. A week later, he had a day off and invited me over again. This time everything was in full blast. He introduced me to the manager, the head waiter, the boss of each gambling room, the several bartenders and then showed me what the thing actually was. The ballroom was crowded, the cabaret was in full swing. There was Harry Lauder singing a melody of Scottish songs; an English actress, Gerty Loftus, sang songs of the English music halls. One of them was, "You'd better pull down the blind." There was a lady from Ziegfeld's Follies. Her name? It was fifty-odd years ago and slips my memory. She sang a catchy song, "She thought that she had lost it at the Astor," but to the dismay of the audience, it turned out to be a fur neckpiece. I learned that their acts were booked from the Keith Circuit and other such agencies. Luisa Tetrazini, famous coloratura soprano, and Nellie Melba, the Australian operatic soprano, were the guests of Alfred and

ATLANTIC HOUSE, 1879
(*Courtesy Joseph M. Connolly*)

Mrs. DiPisa, proprietors of the nearby Villa Napoli. Mrs. DiPisa, herself a noted opera singer, brought them over to the Rockland House where they performed for a crowded ballroom.

George M. Cohan and John McCormack sang here. Among the guests were Chauncy M. Depew, Alfred E. Smith, when he was a New York State Assemblyman, President Grover Cleveland and hundreds of others. I was shown the large billiard room and a smaller room with one billiard table and three tiers of plush bleachers, where admission was charged to see match contests between the foremost billiard players of the world.

The Atlantic House, situated on the top of Atlantic Hill, an imposing structure, was the other of the two largest hotels. A huge wooden structure with several tall towers above the main building, it was founded in 1877 by John L. Damon, and under his administration and that of his son, J. Linfield Damon, was added to until it assumed big proportions. The Damons also owned several cottages which made up the compound. One of them was occupied for one summer by Wallis Simpson, who later became the Duchess of Windsor.

There were 174 guest rooms in the building and many private dining rooms, rooms for roulette and other gambling devices, a huge ballroom for dancing and cabaret, ornate halls and several bars mostly finished in mahogany; even the veranda chairs and tables were mahogany. In the ornate dining hall there were the most elaborate menus that anyone could imagine. The kitchen was very large and equipped to accommodate chefs from four different foreign countries – Germany, France, Italy and China – each trained to the letter to prepare the delicacies of his native land. It was one of the most exclusive hostelries in the country. The rates were fifteen to twenty dollars a day, at the time when the boat fare from Boston to New York was $2.25. You had to

FRONT VIEW OF THE VILLA NAPOLI, 1912
(Courtesy Arthur L. Hurley)

have a certain blood type before you were allowed in the place at all. A long stairway extended from the hotel to the private bathhouse on the sand.

A friend of mine, Edward Gibbons from the next town of Hingham, whose father was a caretaker, told me that Enrico Caruso gave two performances there shortly after the turn of the century, and in 1891, Sarah Bernhardt (Divine Sarah), famous French actress, was a guest there for a week during a tour of the United States. President William McKinley stayed there, too.

To get an idea of the size of these two hotels if might be pointed out that the guest rooms were more than twice as big as the average guest rooms in present-day hotels. It's probably impossible to obtain any of the guest-register books, and it's just as well, because those of today would never believe the long list of famous personalities that have come and gone.

All the hotels and inns that dotted Nantasket in the Gay Nineties are gone, and only the Worrick Mansion still stands at the south end of the beach. William Worrick opened a public house in 1826, and called it "The Sportsman." This old-time inn was the resort of Daniel Webster and other distinguished men during their presidencies of Adams, Jackson and Tyler. They talked about the Hunkers, Barn-burners, Locofocos and other long defunct political parties. In 1867, this old Tavern passed into the hands of Mr. Arthur Pickering of Boston. Later it was owned and used as a summer home by George L. Damon of Boston, a wealthy manufacturer of safes and bank vaults. He occupied it for some twenty-five years. There have been many owners since then. In the intervening years, till World War I, gambling flourished. The place passed through many hands until it was taken over, in 1939, by Jack Eastman. Upon his passing, it was run by his widow, Ann Eastman, and is now operated by his daughter, Dorothy and her husband, Harold Dimond, who run it as a highly respected place, catering to wedding receptions, banquets, class reunions and other social affairs.

The Villa Napoli was formerly the summer estate of the late R.H. Stearns, head of the Boston department store by the same name. It became the property of Alfred DiPisa in the early nineties. He remodeled and enlarged the place into a spacious and beautiful summer hotel. He was at the time proprietor of the Hotel Napoli in Boston. It was later taken over by Frank McPeak and known as McPeak's Shore Gardens. Their gambling rooms and excellent dining hall were similar to other hotels.

The Pemberton Hotel and the Nantasket Hotel with its Rockland Cafe under the same management, noted for their shore dinners along with D.O. Wade's famous clambake, were in existence in the late 1880's and were located close to the head of the steamboat landing and railroad station. With icebox refrigeration in those days, the food would not keep as well, so every Monday, from what was left over from Sunday, D.O. Wade prepared a big dinner with all the fixings for groups of needy children from Boston and paid their way down and back on the Nantasket boats. The clambake was later moved to Nantasket Point, now known as Sunset Point.

The nearby Putnam House in the middle '90's was operated for a short time by John Sweeney and Michael H. Burns. Sweeney took over the Cleveland House and Burns, the Pacific House, both located a little south from the Atlantic House.

The Pacific House was built in 1884. It had various owners up till Burns took the place over from L.E. Bova in 1903. At that time this area was the shoemaking center of the country. The shoemakers played a gambling game called "Props." They were small shells filled with sealing wax and so prepared that it was just about even whether they would fall on the shell or the wax side. They were made by the shoemakers and were the size of a dime. Burns had many friends from the shoe shops who came to the Pacific House, so he provided and equipped a room for them to play in, and also provided the gamekeeper. The house did not bank the game. The

NANTASKET HOTEL, 1879
(Courtesy Francis P. Goulart)

HOTEL PEMBERTON AND WHARF, 1914

(Courtesy R. Loren Graham)

players banked themselves. Four shells or props were used and when they were tossed on the table they came up either nicks (even) or outs (odd). One throw and it was all over. It became known far and wide as the world's fastest and squarest game – no percentage either way. All the house took was 5% of every third pass. It did not take long for the game to catch on and in a couple of months it was going full blast and kept going until Props, Mike Burns and the Pacific House were known throughout most of the country. The prop game flourished for years. However, Burns never learned to save, and he never wanted to. He made a fortune and he spent it as he made it. He was a soft touch for his friends and he had thousands. I never knew of one he ever turned down. Anyone who had a little too much was always provided with a cab to take him home.

In 1914, he left the Pacific House to take over the Oakland House at the other end of the beach. He brought the thriving prop game with him. It was his game and no one else's.

Burns was a veteran of the Indian Wars. He served for three and a half years in the Black Hills and Badlands of the Dakotas, with Company A of the Fifth United States Cavalry against the Cheyenne and Sioux Indians, led by Chiefs Red Cloud, Crazy Horse and Sitting Bull.

Starting before World War I, Burns was host each year in May to the Nelson A. Miles Camp of Indian War Veterans of Roxbury. Burns somehow took a liking to me and invited me as his guest to these banquets. There were about forty-five in the group at the first outing. Lt. General Nelson A. Miles always came with his Indian War veterans. An interesting personality, in his youth he had been a clerk in a Boston store. At the outbreak of the Civil War, he entered the Army as a Lieutenant in the 22nd Massachusetts Regiment. He was with McClellan in the peninsular campaign and remained with the Army of the Potomac constantly until the close of the war. He came out with the rank of Major General of

of the war he was made a Colonel of
Army. He was promoted repeatedly
ie rank of Lieutenant General. Miles'
of an Indian fighter. From 1874 to
heyennes, Comanches, Sioux and
eat Plains country, extending from
e also served with distinction in the
of 1898. His son, Franklin, who was
udge of the Roxbury District Court.
and from listening to him, I learned
history than I ever learned in the
vay in 1925 at the age of eighty-six.
He said many times that Burns was one of the finest soldiers
he had ever known. One of the Indian fighters was a piano
player, and it was a thrill to hear them all sing, "Pretty Red
Wing," "Pony Boy," and other songs of the western plains.
As the years passed, their number dwindled until somewhere
in the 1930's I was at the annual banquet when only three of
them could come. Burns and I sat at a table in the corner of
the dining room with the three feeble Indian fighters that
were left. Burns provided the dinner and a few drinks. Then
we helped them to the car to take them home. It was plain
that this was the last banquet. I shook hands with them and
stepped back. Burns helped them into the car and leaned in to
say goodbye. He stepped back and closed the door. He
waved and a feeble wave came back as the car pulled away. I
never thought Mike Burns would cry, but he did that day. He
didn't say a word to anyone. He put his straw hat on, walked
to the back of the hotel, went up to his room and stayed
there the rest of the evening.

He never forgot his old comrades of the Indian wars. He
was their idol. He was an interesting and lovable character.
His mannerisms, the way he talked and moved his hands, his
walk, the way he dressed and his humor were all peculiar to
himself. His word was better than the notarized signature of

most anyone else. He was as much a part of Nantasket as the white sand on the beach. This place will never see the likes of him again. The era that molded him isn't here anymore.

The name of the Oakland House has been changed to Mike Burns Inn. His widow passed away in April, 1967, in her home just behind the inn, at the age of ninety-two. The proprietor is their son Michael R. Burns. The place has all been remodeled and caters to social gatherings, church affairs and wedding parties. It is one of the nicer places on the beach.

The three-mile-long white sandy beach sweeps around in a majestic curve, framed in at both ends by high rocks. It is one of the finest beaches on the Atlantic seaboard. Along this stretch of beach, there were fifty or more smaller hotels and barrooms all carrying on the same type of business.

They were not arrested for indecent exposure.

III

PARAGON PARK

Paragon Park was built in 1905 when the Nantasket Beach property near the Rockland House was bought. The lagoon and gondola canals were dug and construction started by Eastern Park Construction Company owned by a group of Boston capitalists; among them the late George A. Dodge, manager for fifteen years, was the most widely known. The expense of running the huge plant sometimes made it difficult for the owners to make a profit.

In the fall of 1906, a committee of three, appointed by 175 creditors, investigated the affairs of the park which had lost $32,000 that summer; but George A. Dodge continued to own the plant. The park was taken over in 1920 by David Stone and Albert Golden who had concessions in the park for several years before they acquired the property.

The original park was an imposing structure. The huge Palm Garden steeple top with its ornate bandstand jetted out over the Lagoon. The 150-foot tower in the center, the massive entrance on Nantasket Avenue, the entire park was rimmed with huge scenic productions – "The Johnstown Flood" of 1889, which wiped out the city of Johnstown, Pa. with a loss of over 2,000 lives; "Mysterious Asia and the streets of Cairo"; the entire production cast of dancing girls, scenery and all were brought over here from Cairo, Egypt. "From Hades to Paradise" was another huge production. It's not known that the cast was brought in from those two places. The gondolas were brought from Italy as were the gondoliers who propelled them around the big lagoon as they sang the songs of the waterways of their native Venice.

ENTRANCE OF PARAGON PARK, 1905
(Courtesy R. Loren Graham)

INTERIOR VIEW OF PARAGON PARK SHOWING
ELECTRIC TOWER AND LAGOON, 1908
(Courtesy R. Loren Graham)

The camels and camel drivers that gave rides around the park were brought here from Egypt. The Japanese in the Japanese Village all came here from Tokyo. Inside the circular lagoon was a huge centerpiece of flowerbeds and shrubberies, meticulously cared for. The Wild West show in the wide area behind the Palm Garden was made up of cowboys from 101 Ranch, Oklahoma, and full-blooded Indians from that area who cooked on stone fires, washed their clothes on wet stones, lived in wigwams and slept on blankets spread on the ground. It was quite a sight to see the Indians coming to church on Sunday morning, in their full regalia of deerskins, beads and feathers, the squaws walking behind with the papooses strapped to their backs.

There were many other attractions – Bostock's wild animal show with its one-ring circus, the coal mines and scenic railway, coupled with the finest outdoor attractions, at that time, in the world.

There have been as many as a dozen fires since the park was first built. The two worst were in the fall of 1916 and that of March 28th, 1923, that destroyed most of the park and fifty homes. The tower was blown down in a heavy wind gale in 1916. The succession of fires wrought such destruction that the only thing that is left of the old park is the circle swing. Everything else is gone. There is no intent to downgrade the park of today, but in all truthfulness, it bears no resemblance whatever to the Paragon Park of sixty years ago.

Chute the Chuter at the foot of Atlantic Hill, Nantasket Beach, 1895
(Courtesy Francis P. Goulart)

Steam operated See-Saw at the foot of Atlantic Hill, Nantasket Beach,
1894   *(Courtesy Francis P. Goulart)*

INTERIOR VIEW OF PARAGON PARK, 1908
(Courtesy R. Loren Graham)

S. S. MYLES STANDISH, NANTASKET LINE

S. S. NANTASKET, NANTASKET LINE

S. S. BETTY ALDEN, NANTASKET LINE

IV

TRANSPORTATION

From the 1870's to shortly before World War I, the transportation to and from Nantasket was by boat, train and trolley car.

The Nantasket Beach Steamboat Company, formerly the Boston and Hingham Steamboat Company, carried the bulk of the passenger traffic between Boston and Nantasket. There were eleven steamers in the fleet: *Myles Standish, Rose Standish, John Alden, Betty Alden, Old Colony, Plymouth, Mary Chilton, Governor Andrew, Mayflower, South Shore* and *Nantasket.* They were all the same design, side paddle and steam driven. It was hard to tell one from another without looking at the name on the side and bow. Each was about 195 feet long with a 33-foot beam. Each was capable of carrying 2,000 passengers. They were luxury boats, plush carpeting, mahogany staircases and paneling, mahogany chairs with velvet seats and backs. The captain's quarters were on the top deck just behind the pilot house. The purser's and the mate's room was on the second deck forward and on each side, below decks was a spacious galley where the crew's meals were prepared and served, and clean quarters where the crew slept. Comfortable benches rimmed each boat all around the decks and camp stools were provided on crowded days for those unable to get seats. Each boat, equipped with a huge generator, provided its own electricity and each had its own steam heating system.

The boats ran each summer from the 19yh of April to the 12th of October. It was always the custom of the company to keep all of its captains, pilots, pursers and other help the year-round. At the end of the season extra help was put on.

Each vessel was completely reconditioned. The paint was taken off down to the wood and two new coats put on. Each was taken to dry dock, the paint taken off, reconditioned and repainted below the water line. The company owned and maintained their own supply pier near Pemberton. The three beautiful wharfs at Nantasket, Nantasket Point and Pemberton were reconditioned and repainted each year. Frederick L. Lane, general manager and treasurer of the line, often stated, "I have always been proud of our record of minor accidents and the fact that the steamers on our line have never lost a life." Very few under sixty years of age can remember what a luxury line that really was. The Nantasket Beach Steamboat Company was the finest asset Nantasket has ever had.

The South Shore branch of the Old Colony Railroad connected with the main line at Braintree and ran through the south shore to Plymouth. The Nantasket Beach Railroad started in the 1870's from the South Shore branch at Nantasket Junction and ran through Nantasket along the ocean front to Pemberton. The branch was electrified by overhead wires in 1895, and in 1896 the first use of the third rail by a surface railroad in the United States was on the Nantasket Beach Railroad's extension to Eat Weymouth and Braintree. It was a delightful ride on the electric trains and they were very heavily patronized. Their largest station was at the head of the Nantasket Steamboat wharf.

The trolley lines ran from Nantasket to Boston direct, and also connected with other lines from all over southeastern Massachusetts. They were very heavily patronized. Their terminal was also at the head of the wharf. Large horse-drawn barges (like our busses) provided free transportation to and from the Rockland House, Atlantic House and others of the large hotels. The head of the wharf, being the terminal for all three forms of transportation, made that area the most congested on the beachfront. Many horse-drawn hackneys, to transport patrons for a small charge to whatever place they wished, were ready and waiting.

For the forty-odd-years before World War I, the only place licensed for the sale of liquor from Boston to the tip of Provincetown, was Nantasket. It was an oasis, if there ever was one, for all of southeastern Massachusetts. There were for the most time, two year-round licenses and a few summer permits. The summer licenses kept open year-round, all others kept open all year with no license at all. As long as they went along with the local political machine, nobody bothered them.

As soon as the trolley car conductors and motormen hit the beach, the way they guzzled down beer and booze, it's a damn wonder the cars stayed on the tracks at all. Quite often they didn't.

NANTASKET WHARF

Nantasket Wharf of the Nantasket Beach Steamboat Company with Electric Train Station in background. Rockland Cafe and Nantasket Hotel in far background, 1898.

STEAMBOAT INTERIOR

Saloon deck S. S. Rose Standish, Nantasket Line. The interior of all eleven steamers were finished alike.

S. S. MAYFLOWER

The S. S. Mayflower in its final resting place at the entrance of the beach. Now used as a night club and dance casino, 1950.

(Courtesy R. Loren Graham)

ELECTRIC TRAINS NANTASKET RAILROAD, 1895
(Courtesy R. Loren Graham)

NANTASKET RAILROAD THIRD RAIL, 1896
(Courtesy Joseph M. Connolly)

V

CON GAMES AND THE PICKPOCKET

It was mostly in this congested area that the con men and pickpockets were allowed to operate. I remember two flim-flam games in particular, the shell game and three-card monte. Each was played on a small shelf suspended by a strap from the operator's shoulders.

The shell game was played with three half-walnut shells and a pea. The customer was given the pea and asked to put it under one of the shells. The operator would move the shells slowly back and forth, then ask the customer to bet that he could pick out the shell that the pea was under. He couldn't win because the pea wasn't under any shell but skillfully concealed in the crease of the operator's little finger. The pea, of course, would be under the shell that the operator picked up.

Three-card monte was played about the same way as the shell game, with three playing cards instead of shells face down on the board. The customer would pick up one card, let everybody look at it, then place it back on the board. The operator would slowly shift the cards around and then let the customer make a bet that he could pick out his card. He had no chance to win. They would let the customer win every once in a while to keep up the interest.

These and many other kinds of flim-flam games were operating all over the place, on the beach sand, the hotel verandas, sidewalks, streets, at the wharf and railroad termi-nal. They paid no attention to the police and the police paid no attention to them.

In the decade before the turn of the century, Nantasket was the pickpocket's paradise. They preyed on those who were coming to the beach as they came off the boats, trains and trolley cars. They knew there was not much money in the pockets of those who were going home. They also operated at an arcade near the Rockland Cafe across the street from the terminal. Inside the arcade were signs "Beware of the Pickpockets." The signs were put there by the pickpockets themselves. When a man came through the door and his eyes spotted the sign, instinct moved his hand to where his wallet was. That's all the pickpocket wanted to know.

There were scenes at the head of the wharf that would make you sick. Sunday school teachers with fifteen or twenty tots, bringing nickels and pennies in, for months having saved for their excursion on the boat to Nantasket. When she got off the boat with them and before she left the wharf her pocketbook and all the money would be gone. The same thing was happening to mothers bringing their children for the boat ride to the beach. Many of their victims were old ladies who were not bothering anyone and never expected to be bothered. Men, who looked to see what time it was, couldn't find their watches. These were constant and daily occurrences.

There was a deep well near Wade's Clambake, close to the steamboat wharf, that had been abandoned and covered over. They decided to reactivate the well. They shoveled off about a foot of gravel and found that the well was fully filled with empty wallets, billfolds, and pocketbooks. There was a forty-foot cabin boat high and dry on the beach, right close to the boat wharf. It had been badly damaged in a storm. Its large cabin was padlocked. There was a round glass porthole on the side in which the glass was broken. It was on the beach for four years before it was broken up and taken away. When they broke into the cabin they found it to be stuffed to the roof with empty pocketbooks. Underneath the hotel verandas and catch basins were other areas for the disposal of empty wallets.

The pickpockets were forbidden to operate on the boats, trains and trolleys and those lines were very good, the Nantasket steamers in particular, at providing passage home for the pickpockets' victims, stranded on the beach.

The pickpockets were given strict orders by the police to throw the empty wallets in certain designated places so there would be no tell-tale evidence laying around, to show what was going on. The police would honor no complaints. The only ones they bothered were those who interfered with the con men and the pickpockets.

Anyone who had his pockets picked would be reluctant to admit it. Those who did complain would not give their names as shown in the following article in the *Quincy Ledger of Monday, July 19, 1897:*

"Quincy Man Robbed – Pocket Picked at Nantasket

"One of our citizens had his pocketbook taken from his pants pocket, yesterday afternoon while waiting to purchase a ticket to East Weymouth.

"The affair would not have been made public probably, but he afterwards leaned that it was a common occurrence and he wished to warn our citizens who visited the noted summer resort to be on their guard.

"The facts are these: About six o'clock, the unfortunate gentleman went to the station to purchase a ticket to East Weymouth. On arriving there, a large number were standing around the depot waiting for a train, and many were in the passageway which is long and narrow, leading to the ticket office. As it was about time for a train he did not pay particular attention to the crowd, but went for a ticket. As the crowd moved very slowly, it was some minutes before he was able to get to the window. On purchasing his ticket with some change he had in his vest pocket, he moved back and discovered at once before leaving the station, that his wallet was gone. It contained a few dollars in bills, some checks and other papers of value.

"Instead of leaving on the train, he waited until after the crowd was gone, and then told the ticket seller and asked him if there was any officer there whom he could notify. The agent told him it would be of little use as it was a common occurrence, sometimes as many as twenty a day were stolen. If the agent's statement was true the railroad company should have posted notices warning their patrons to beware of pickpockets and also have detectives there to protect the people and arrest the rascals.

"The unfortunate man noticed in front of him a person who seemed to be in no hurry to move along, and when he got up to the window the man did not purchase any ticket or even ask for any or show any signs that he wanted a ticket. Probably he was in league with one or two other pals who did the work."

The human is proud. He wants to give the impression that he is brighter than he really is. If his pocket is picked he will never divulge it. He wants others to know that he is too smart to have that happen to him. It will never be found out from the victims.

The observation of one ticket seller, and there were several others, that sometimes as many as twenty a day were stolen, coupled with the amazing number of empty pocketbooks found, was mute evidence that Nantasket in the "Gay Nineties" was truly a pickpocket's paradise.

At that time John Irwin operated a cafe and picnic ground on Peddocks Island just off the tip of the town. An Irish Society hired the picnic grounds for their annual outing. The pickpockets thought that was a good place to work. After the barrels were rolled out and the members were feeling fairly decent, a pickpocket walked up and punched an Irishman in the mouth, then stepped back so another Irishman was closer than he was. The one he hit hauled off and pasted the first face he saw and the whole picnic grounds was in the hell of a free-for-all. When the battle finally cooled off, most of the Irishmen's watches and wallets were gone. The Irish Society learned their lesson and learned it well.

They came back the next summer for their annual outing. This time they were slow in rolling out the barrel. They carefully counted noses. They found out that there were nine strangers in their midst. They watched carefully for the same thing to happen, and sure enough it did. One of the pickpockets punched an Irishman in the face. This time they nailed the pickpocket, gave him an unmerciful beating and dragged him away. Aside from the operators of the cafe, as near as was known, the only ones to leave the island alive were the members of the Irish Society. Three of the pickpockets' bodies were washed ashore on Nantasket beach and no one ever found out what happened to the other six.

VI

HOUSES OF ILL REPUTE

The beach was dotted with houses of prostitution. Some of the better-known places were The Ginger Bread, the Riding Academy, The Red Top Inn, The Pussy Willow, Jennies' Place and The Cuckoo's Nest.

The Cuckoo's Nest opened its doors for business without making the necessary arrangements with the chairman of the Board of Selectmen. He got wind of it and told the Chief of Police to find out what was going on down there. The Chief sent one of his officers down to investigate. An hour and a half went by and he didn't come back. He sent a second officer down and he didn't come back. He sent a third officer down for the other two and he didn't come back. Then the Chief went down and found the three of them in the joint. The Chief might have stayed there himself, only there would have been no one on the desk. He told them to put their clothes on and "get to hell out of here."

When they got back to the station the Chief gave them hell for staying there so long, but they explained they were trying to give a detailed and comprehensive report.

The proprietress immediately completed arrangements with the chairman and was given the "go ahead." He thought the place must be pretty good to gather in over half the police force before it was "officially" in business.

A Selectman was a constant visitor to the Mistress of a questionable house across the street from his home. After his visits became too conspicuous, he built a house for her about a half mile away. Every evening he could be seen walking over to her new place to "check and see if everything was all right."

On September 4th, 1897, four women were arrested by the police for keeping houses of ill repute and were fined sixty dollars each in the Hingham District Court. The Chief said the raids were made to "clean up the beach." It was later learned that the houses were far in arrears in their payments to the town officials.

The following article, in part, appeared in the *Hull Beacon* of July 24, 1897:

"The proprietors of the big hotels are losing business and Nantasket is fast becoming a second Coney Island with its beer gardens and fake shows. What the future of the beach will be unless some determined stand to check the fake crowd, the abusers of licenses and keepers of houses of ill fame that abound, anyone can predict."

Of the volume of letters that poured into the newspaper the following letter was published in the *Hull Beacon* of July 31, 1897:

"'Your article in last week's paper was right to the point and I sincerely hope you will keep at these illegal rum sellers and keepers of houses of ill repute and other dens of evil until everyone is driven away. That the beach is going backward in its moral tone is plainly seen by us cottagers. I think by getting together we can speedily find a way to kill these evils.

July 26, 1897 Signed

Jerusalem Road.'"

The *Hull Beacon* was a clean and proud newspaper and in a later edition stated that they would not print any more of the filth that was going on at Nantasket Beach.

News Items of the Time

The following article appeared in the *Boston Traveler* on Saturday, August 21, 1897:

"POLICE OWN THE BEACH

"Corruption Flourishes on Nantasket Sands

"Poo Bah Rulers

"Better to Take Money from Liquor Sellers

"Than it is to 'License'

"The Hull police had a ball last night in the Nantasket Dance Hall, and thereby hangs a tale.

"It was a wild and riotous time. There were frequent excursions over the plank walk to the Tivoli, some of them headed by Chief John Mitchell in person, and the bar, which was kept open until 3 o'clock in spite of the so-called police regulations, was generously patronized by Chief Mitchell and his men. Their feminine companions were served on the piazza and in the private room upstairs, and did a rushing business, I understand, until 4 o'clock this morning. All regular patrons of the hotel were barred out after 10 o'clock. Strangers, innocently supposing that a hotel was obliged to serve food and lodging to respectable applicants, were refused admission to every part of the house except the bar, which as I have said, was wide open to the general public until after 3 o'clock. All the hotels along the beach, not only the Nantasket, but Jones' Surfside House, Joe Lannon's Fairhaven, the Standish, the Ocean House and Taylor's, the Waveland and others along the beach were all closed early and ordinary guests refused accommodation because the Hull Police have many balls; in fact, each and every member of the force has 'balls' without number all day long and far into the night, and good reason why.

"The town of Hull, which includes Nantasket, is a sort of private corporation. John Smith is the chairman of the Board of Selectmen. John is also superintendent of streets, and, by strange coincidence, John does almost all the teaming for the town of Hull. John makes out his bills for teaming, which are generous, addresses them to himself, as chairman of the Board of Selectmen, and O.K.'s them as superintendent of streets. John has a snap, and he knows it. And that is not all he gets out of it. His sister married John Mitchell, and John Mitchell is chief of police, and, somehow or other the officials at Hull and Nantasket find it more profitable to license a few saloons and let the many run without any license at all. Of course, the many, that is those who have no license, or at best, a beer license, have to fix 'somebody.' That 'somebody' ought not to be hard to find. Smith is chairman of the Board of Selectmen, and his brother-in-law, John Mitchell, is chief of police. Mitchell has a willing crowd. There are usually five policemen in Hull the year round who live on the inhabitants. They triple that number during the summer time, and the hotels all have their special officers. These men are recruited from behind the bars and in front of the theatres of Boston.

"There are other selectmen down at Hull also. There is Captain Galiano of the *Governor Andrew* of the Nantasket line. The captain is taking care of his brother or cousin, who is Officer Galiano of the Hull police. Then there is Jeffries. Jeffries is a selectman. He used to be ticket agent of the Nantasket station of the New York, New Haven & Hartford railroad, but finds it more profitable now to attend solely to his business as selectman. His brother is now the division superintendent of the Nantasket division of the New York, New Haven & Hartford railroad. Jeffries also has a few good things in Nantasket, but he does not talk much about them. It is an old saying among the old-fashioned voters of the state, 'as Hull goes so goes the state.' If that is to be the case in the future we may indeed say 'God save the Commonwealth of Massachusetts.'

"John Y. McKane, 'the King of Coney Island,' now serving a sentence in Sing Sing Prison because he was too good to his friends, never in all his palmy days so thoroughly controlled his bailiwick as do the Hull selectmen over that popular stretch of shore from Hull Gut to Black Rock. They own everything and everybody. They sell licenses were they can, and they wink at illegal liquor selling whenever the wink is paid for. They control the street building and the profits thereof. They exact a weekly stipend from every 'fakir' on the beach. They permit their policemen to filch from the pockets of their prisoner, while they filch from the pocket of the taxpayer.

"Why, it was only the other night when one of the Hull policemen singled out one of the many drunken men who staggered forth at late hours from the Hotel Nantasket, followed him up the beach and told him that if he would pay $5, the amount of the fine he would have to pay next morning in court, he would let him go. He did. These Hull policemen are not so much to blame. They know how far they can go. They watch their superiors and do likewise. I saw Chief Mitchell last night walk up to the bar of the Tivoli Hotel three times after 11 o'clock and take a drink; I don't know whether the Chief paid for it, or whether Joe Lannon paid for it. Joe was there, and so were several other keepers of alleged hotels along the beach. It happened last night because of the Tivoli, next to the Nantasket dance hall, happened to be in the position to get all the trade, but that is not usually the case. They usually keep open as long as there is a man on the beach who has money to spend for liquor. A man who goes to Nantasket and knows the ropes can get a drink at any time of the day or night, and he need not know what a sandwich looks like. He can get it at Jones' whose semi-weekly balls are notorious; he can get it at Lannon's; he can get it as Mrs. Woods'; he can get it at the Nantasket; and he can always get it at the Tivoli; and there is not one of the so-called hotels on Nantasket Beach but what sells liquor on Sunday all day, just as they do on weekdays, with the exception only that their customers have to sit down at a table instead of standing up at the bar. Not only do visitors and frequenters of the beach get their liquor without question, or sandwich, but the police in uniform sit down and take their places with the rest. The ball for the Hull police is not the only good thing, although they did make everybody buy tickets except the newspaper men of whom they were afraid.

"They have a good thing all round. They work the drunks; they work the beach 'fakirs'; they work the saloon keepers, who have no licenses and those who have; and they even blackmail the women, who frequent the resorts so thickly scattered along the sands. It was one night when I saw a policeman, a big blonde-moustached policeman, walk up to a group of girls seated on the veranda, in front of the Rockland Café, sit down, put his arm about one of them, and forgetting his duty, gossiped for half an hour. He did not know any of the girls. That same night the big, black-moustached policeman at the Tivoli spent five, supposedly happy minutes, on the merry-go-round nearby. He made a pretty picture. The girl had her arm around his neck and her head on his shoulder. He was puffing a big cigar and seemed to think that he was having a good time. Five *Traveler* reporters were watching him. Ten minutes later he deliberately left his station in front of the veranda door of the hotel, and followed a young girl down the plank walk, who accidentally lifted her dress to high going down the step. These two men are fair samples of the Hull police. Next week the *Traveler* will give some incidents that will prove this, and next week the *Traveler* will probably mention the names of those concerned. But if the abuse of power at Nantasket was confined merely to self-advancement one could understand the reason, but I fail to see how the police profit by committing the nightly holdups, assaults, robberies and crimes of a worse description, which have made Nantasket beach a place to be shunned by every respectable man after the last boat leaves the pier.

"Of course, when a man is held up on the beach, having stayed over from the last boat, he is usually more or less intoxicated, and is naturally ashamed to make public any misfortune that may befall him. It is upon this fear of publicity that the Nantasket Beach thugs prey. And these thugs have a double mission; not only do they, with the consent of the police, rob the visitors both day and night, but before the 1st of May when the count was taken which determined the number of licenses to be issued for the summer, they flocked to the beach from Boston, registered at the numerous alleged hotels which, for that reason and others, get licenses or a tacit permission to sell without a license, and not only count as residents, but actually as voters of the town of Hull. 'As Hull goes, so goes the state.' That is the way Hull goes. The riff-raff, the abandoned men and women of the city are the first to flock to a summer resort where they know the police can be bought and sold. It used to be that way at Crescent Beach. Everybody knows what Crescent Beach used to be. Husbands forbade their wives, parents their children, to visit the place. It is so now at Nantasket, so far as the first statement is concerned. There is more deviltry and general cussedness at Nantasket Beach today than there is in poor old Coney Island.

"There are bathing parties after dark, from which the police studiously keep away, which disgrace civilization. On certain portions of the beach bathing suits are deemed unnecessary. On the more public portions, costumes more scanty than any newspaper dare picture, are an every night sight both among men and women. I don't know whether John Mitchell, Chief of Police, winks at all this, because he has to or because he wants to. Mitchell is a good fellow, a typical Yankee in appearance, of genial whole-souled temperament, loyal to his friends, and generally speaking, a good all-round fellow. So is John Y. McKane. But if it is not Mitchell, or if it is not Mitchell's brother-in-law, the Chairman of the Board of Selectmen, or the Nantasket Steamboat Corporation, of the New York, New Haven & Hartford people, it must be somebody else, because somebody gets the money.

"All this violation of the law, all this illegal liquor selling, all this discrimination at hotels, all these holdups of drunks by the police on the beach after dark, all this general deviltry, is winked at, and somebody is paid to wink, or to make others wink. Why, even the hotel proprietors down there know the dangerous character of the business.

"In Pogie's saloon, on the veranda in front of the Rockland Café, every bartender carries a loaded revolver, and both times I have been there I have seen a revolver hung up behind the cash register. Joe Lannon of the Fairhaven boasts that he hires his waiters because of their fighting ability. It fares ill with the man who protests when he does not get the right change or when he insists on accompanying the women paid hirelings of the hotels, who have induced him to spend his all in rum. It is time that the citizens of Boston, from whom Nantasket Beach gets its prosperity, should look into this matter. It is time that the Metropolitan Park Commission should see fit to rescue this beautiful stretch of beach from the hands of thugs and hand it over to the people. Crescent Beach has been made respectable because the rum sellers, the fast women, the thugs and thieves have been driven out. The same thing can be done at Nantasket."

The following appeared in the *Boston Traveler* one week later, on August 30, 1897:

"DIVES WERE RAIDED

But Little was done at Nantasket

"Was 'TIP' Given?

"Chief Mitchell Says 'We'll Clean Out Dens.'

"TRAVELER *Drove Him to It*

"NANTASKET, Aug. 30 – Driven desperate by the ex-posures in *"The Traveler*, Chief of Police John L. Mitchell and members of his force of Nonpareils raided several of the dens which have been running full blast ever since the season opened.

"The chief had defied public criticism and public indignation until the season had come to a close. He had set himself up as the ruler of Nantasket, and he intended to rule as he pleased. But *The Traveler's* exposure of the rottenness of police affairs at Nantasket proved too much for the man with the rhinoceros hide, and he was forced to make the move he did on Saturday night. It was a rather late move on the chief's part, but better late than never may be said fittingly in this instance.

"Of course, the chief in his talk to the reporters, 'hogged' all the honor of the raid. He threw out his chest, swelled with official importance, formed an expression of righteousness and purity, which didn't seem to fit his face, and then, with a sanctity which would have done credit to the late Mr. Pecksniff, said that he couldn't tell a lie, he knew such things existed, and he had decided to clean them out.

"Of course, the public, including the entire population of Hull and Nantasket Beach, know that it was *The Traveler* that drove the chief into something like action.

"He only partially succeeded, but this is how he tells it:

" 'The first attack was made on the Boston cottage, kept by Ella Bassett, formerly of 1070 Washington Street, Boston, at 12:30. A quantity of whiskey and glassware was captured and George Littleton and Jessie Conley were arrested, charged with unbecoming behavior.

" 'The next move was on the Elliott cottage, kept by Thomas M. Burbeck, where a quantity of liquor was captured.

" 'From this place we proceeded to the Grand View cottage on Sagamore Hill run by Mrs. Frances Griswold, where 20 bottles of beer were confiscated.

" 'Franky must have been warned at the last moment, as other game which we had expected to capture was not found.

" 'By this time the morning was rapidly advancing, and hostilities ceased, but were resumed at noon, when the Putnam House, kept by Seth Reckards, was entered and small quantity of ale was seized.

" 'The next place visited was the Pilgrim House, conducted by William Grant. Here one bottle of whiskey and a small quantity of beer were found.'

"The chief alleges that there is a likeness between him and Davy Crockett. He says he is sure he's right before he goes ahead. It takes the chief a long time to make sure. It seems he wasn't sure until *The Traveler* made him positive. Unlikewise, Davy used to bag his game. The chief was not so successful. He says someone must have given the tip. Well, if the police force is in perfect working order, where did the tip come from?

"It must have come from close to headquarters, for if he did not 'tip' off his men they would not know, and if his men did not know, how could others?

"The chief also says that he has had warrants 'out' for places since July 13. Why were they not served? Did the places pay protection?

"The warrant for the Putnam House, however, was not

sworn out until August 28, three days after it was exposed in *The Traveler.*

"The chief resembles John Y. McKane more than Davy Crockett. Let's hope he'll stop the resemblance before it becomes too marked.

"While the chief has his hand in, he might tackle some others of the dens exposed in *The Traveler.* He says he is going to keep up the good work. He could not do better. He might begin right with the police force – discharge all his men and then resign himself. Then much good might be accomplished if his successor was not appointed by Selectman Smith."

The following is from the *Hull Beacon* of March 4, 1899:

"The chief of police and one of his officers, charged with protecting the illegal sale of liquor on Nantasket Beach, came up in Plymouth Superior Court, Judge Brady presided. The arrest of the chairman of the Board of Selectmen, the Chief of Police and a constable for receiving a bribery of $50 a week from a woman and a man, eleven counts charged against the Police Chief and his constable. Another indictment charges the Chief with receiving $50 on four different occasions from a woman all for the protection of selling illegal liquor."

The concern here is to describe the conditions as they existed at that time. The names of those involved have been purposely left out. The full account of this and many other instance s of its kind can be seen in the newspapers on file at the State Library and the office of Secretary of the Commonwealth, Archives Division, State House, Boston.

Raids by the State Police, across the years proved to be ineffective. In many of these raids they courteously sought the help of the local police. In these cases the State Police for some mysterious reason would find nothing wrong with the places that were raided.

They then inaugurated a series of raids conducted without the knowledge of the local police. Liquor and gambling devices, etc., seized in these raids would be confiscated and a few minutes after the raiding party left the houses would be running wide open again. They operated with a light stock of liquor and dice tables and whatever else was taken could be easily replaced.

The jurisdiction of these cases was in the local courts. The local courts were part of the local society. The judge was friendlier to his neighbors than he was to strangers from outside. When the case came up in court the judge would be a little confused as to what a proprietor was. When he'd ask for the proprietor to step forward, some flunky who cleaned out the spittoons would walk up and fork over the modest fine before the judge would tell him how much it was. The flunky was a big shot for a day when his name appeared in the Boston newspapers as the proprietor of a Nantasket hotel. These fines had already been set aside in the estimated running expenses of the joints that were raided.

When the accounts of these raids would appear in the Boston newspapers the Hull police would pull off a couple of trumped-up raids themselves just to water down the adverse publicity. The Hull police had no civil service or any other protection. They were absolutely at the mercy of the Hull selectmen. If the selectmen wanted to clean Nantasket up, they could have done it in a hurry.

The State Police raids accomplished absolutely nothing. In fact, the joints that were raided on account of the notoriety did far more business than those that were not. A few years back the State Police raided a barroom in the Green Hill section for operating pinball machines. They seized two machines. To the old-timers that was like raiding the Parent Teachers Association. The point here is a few minutes after the raid and before the booking exercises were over, two other machines were installed and the place was doing business just the same. State Police raids are just a waste of time.

An interesting sidelight: A local lady was in the place when it was raided. She had inhaled a few and consented to go with the police and pose as the proprietor. It was the hottest day of the summer and she was scantily dressed, as it later turned out. A news photographer started to take her picture out in front of the police station. Just before the camera was snapped, she drew her skirt up over her face and head. I'm sure you'll pardon me if I have no comment on why the picture was never developed.

Here in the late nineties was a town government that condoned, encouraged and protected illegal liquor sales, rampant gambling, prostitution, con games and pickpockets, and the States Police was unable to do a thing about it. Hell had really broken loose in Nantasket. The people all over Massachusetts were up in arms. The resentment ran so high that complaints were lodged with the state agencies and with the federal government. Some requests were made to have the town occupied by the armed forces of the United States, but the federal government took the position that it was the state's responsibility.

On February 3, 1899, a bill was introduced in the legislature by Miss Floretta Vining, a prominent newspaperwoman, and others for the Metropolitan Park Commission to take over the entire beach from end to end. That bill fell through.

From the *Hull Beacon* of February 11, 1899:

"A bill was filed in the legislature to establish a board of police for the Town of Hull. The bill was not directed at the policeman or the chief but a movement to deprive the selectmen of the prerogatives of granting licenses and appointing police service on Nantasket beach, whether good or bad will not be argued against the officers but the Board of Selectmen as their legal supervisors are practicably responsible for any inefficient service if it existed. Origin of the bill was attributed to Mr. Edward A. Knight because his name headed the list, but while he disclaimed authorship of the bill, he believed in the petition and signed it. There were several other signers." (This bill also fell through.)

Public indignation spread through Boston and all over eastern Massachusetts and penetrated the legislature as well. Then on April 24, 1899, another bill was introduced in the legislature for the Metropolitan Park Commission to take Nantasket Beach as a park reservation, limiting the sum to be paid at $600,000, distance on the beach to be taken 5600 feet. Strait's Pond and adjacent waters were included in the bill. No liquor licenses to be granted within 400 feet of the reservation.

When the hearings were held before the Ways and Means Committee and the Committee on Metropolitan Affairs, the State House corridors were so crowded that the hearings were shifted to the State House Auditorium from the hearing rooms. In the bill that was finally acted on, the clause "Straits Pond and adjacent waters" was stricken out.

The final act provided for an area of the beachfront not exceeding 5600 feet in length, no sale of intoxicating liquor, and no liquor licenses to be granted within 400 feet of the land taken. The measure was passed and enacted into law and became Chapter 464, Acts of 1899, approved June 2, 1899, and later in Chapter 421, Acts of 1900, the Metropolitan Park Commission took over Nantasket Avenue and roads and public ways that abut on the property taken. And finally, the State of Massachusetts took over complete ownership, supervision and policing, a mile stretch, the wildest part of the beach. All liquor sales were barred on the reservation and for four hundred feet more in all directions, gambling was prohibited, the con men and pickpockets were routed, and the bathers on the beach started to behave like ladies and gentlemen. And so, for that golden mile of beach front, the very heart of Old Nantasket, the honeymoon was over.

For the next decade the big hotels were heavily patronized, the Nantasket Steamboats ran to capacity, the electric trains and trolley car traffic was very heavy. Paragon Park and the outside amusements were crowded. Up to this time as the steamboats became unserviceable they were replaced with new ones by the same name.

VII

THE OLD ORDER CHANGETH

During the ten years through World War I, the rapidly increasing growth of the automobile was beginning to make its impact on the American economy. As travel by motor car increased there was a correspondent decline on other modes of transportation. Worn-out steamboats were not replaced. The patronage of the big hotels began to fall off. In 1918, the trolley cars were discontinued. Shortly after, the electric trains stopped running.

By this time, the rapid increase in motor car production was putting the finishing touches on the last remaining means of transportation. On May 26, 1927, the Ford Motor Company produced the fifteen millionth model "T" car. On that memorable occasion, Henry Ford met Calvin Coolidge. They shook hands. Ford said, "I suppose Mr. President you shook the hands of half the people of this country." He said, "Yes, and you shook the shit out of the other half."

On Thanksgiving Day afternoon, November, 1929, with the remaining six of the original ten steamers of the Nantasket Beach Line, *Mayflower*, *Nantasket*, *Old Colony*, *Mary Chilton*, *Betty Alden* and *Rose Standish* tied up in a semicircle around the Nantasket Pier, fire broke out on the wharf and with a forty mile an hour wind, quickly spread to three of the six steamers. In short time two others were ablaze. Firemen with axes came in close enough to cut the ropes holding the *Mayflower* to the wharf and the big boat drifted away from the fire. It had caught twice. Each time the fire was put out.

The *Mayflower* was burned about the upper deck and bow with a loss of $2500. The other five steamers were totally destroyed and sank to the bottom, with an estimated loss of over one million dollars. The damage to the pier was set at $10,000. The men's section of the state bathhouse was burned with a loss of $25,000. Eight homes and the steeple of the church of St. Mary of the Assumption, a half-mile away, caught fire. The flames were quickly extinguished and the damage slight. These figures are rather confusing; a million dollar loss then would be five million in today's economy.

The tugboat *Mars* of the Boston Towboat Company, ordered to the scene by the Nantasket Steamboat Company, towed the *Mayflower* safely to the steamboat supply pier at Pemberton where she was tied up. In a few short years following the fire, the Nantasket Steamboat Company, with its once resplendent steamers, floundered and died.

Twenty years ago the *Mayflower*, the last remaining steamboat of the old Nantasket Line, out of use for years and tied up to the wharf, was towed across the waters of the bay to her final resting place up on dry land at the entrance to the beach. It is now used as a nightclub and dance casino and named the *Showboat Mayflower*.

One beautiful evening, when the line was in its heyday, I slipped onto the boat to take a ride up to Boston and back. Shortly after the boat started, I hit up a conversation with a delightful young lady up on the moonlit deck. We talked, laughed and whispered sweet nothings all the way to Boston. When we got off the boat, she grabbed me around the neck, her feet dangling a foot off the ground. She gave me three tremendous kisses, with the last one she bit my lip and broke the rim of my sailor straw hat. She let go of my neck, slid down and in a moment she was lost in the crowd. I never saw her again. It was ten minutes before the next boat back, so when my brain stopped whirling I stepped over to a barroom across the street to get a pick-me-up for the trip back home. Two days later I got a letter from her, telling me how enchanting the boat ride was. At the bottom of the letter she wrote "oceans of love, a kiss on each wave and a big storm at sea." It must have been the boat ride. I never paralyzed any other girl in my life like that.

When the last boat pulled away from the wharf and faded away in the mist, it left behind a nostalgia hard to understand. Moist eyes, sad hearts. Gone were the moonbeams on the water, the soft ocean breezes, tingling romance, the soothing moon and for old and young alike, fond memories of days that were gone.

The growth of the automobile made the same destructive impact on the big hotels as it made on the steamboats, electric trains and trolley lines. Business was falling off. They were losing money fast.

In a wild swirling snowstorm of February 4, 1916, the big Rockland House was burned to the ground. A caretaker had been at the hotel all winter and used the kitchen and back part of the hotel for living quarters; that is where the fire started. No cause for the fire could be given by the firemen or the caretaker, although the "accident" could never have happened under more perfect conditions.

On January 7, 1927, the Atlantic House, for more than two generations the most famous summer hotel in New England, was destroyed by fire in less than an hour. The hotel was founded in 1877, by John L. Damon. Guests came from all over the world and many celebrities have slept beneath its roof. In 1924, the Damon interests sold out to John Crowley of Quincy, but there was some trouble over littoral rights and the matter had been pending in the courts. The *Boston Globe* stated at the time that the cause of the fire was unknown. Miss Mary Abrams, caretaker of the property, stated that she made her round of the buildings late in the afternoon and there was nothing that could have caused the fire. The electricity was shut off when the hotel closed, the day after Labor Day, and there had been no heating or cooking fire of any description in the building since then.

One summer day four years ago, I was sitting on my

veranda when an old gangster friend of mine came walking along the sidewalk. I hadn't seen him in years, so we shook hands. He pulled a chair over and we sat down. He was a likeable old smoothy and fun to talk with. We talked about old times on the beach and went into a most interesting conversation. He started to talk about the Atlantic House. I interrupted him a couple of times but he kept coming back to the Atlantic House. I breathed along and listened. He went into a detailed account of the 1927 fire. I had a copy of the *Boston Globe* of January 8, 1927, that gave a complete and detailed story, but he gave me far more information than the *Globe* did. I asked him, "How do you know so much about the Atlantic House fire?" He said, "I ought to know, I was the one that set it."

He told me that he and another man who helped him and drove the car, kept a very close watch on the caretaker and the last round she made was three days before the fire, and not on the afternoon of the fire as stated in the *Boston Globe*. They did not use the stairway leading from the bath-house on the sand to the hotel. They crawled over the rocks and up the knoll on the north end of the hotel. There was a door in the latticework enclosure under the veranda where a pile of empty wooden bushel boxes was stacked up. A week before the fire they brought four five-gallon milk cans full of gasoline and covered them over with the boxes. They waited for the perfect night. On January 7th, freezing cold with a northwest gale blowing off the ocean at 9 o'clock at night, they crawled over the rocks and the knoll, went under the veranda, sprinkled the contents of the milk cans all over the boxes and with a twenty-two foot bamboo pole, with gas-oline soaked rags tied to the tip end, they lit the tip and poked the pole through the partly open door so they would not get burned from the gasoline-flash. They came down over the knoll, over the rocks, across the sand and over the M.D.C. parking area and off they went. He told me they drove a couple of miles toward Hingham, tuned around, came back and watched the place burn down from their car in the same parking area. He never told me why he set the fire. Those fellows tell you what they want you to know and no more. I asked him if I could tell the story. He told me that I could. Although it happened forty years ago, he made me promise never to use his name in connection with the fire.

I'll never mention his name for two reasons: one, I gave him my word of honor that I wouldn't, and the other, if I did I would probably get the Swiss cheese treatment. His name and address is in the Boston telephone directory. His partner passed away eleven years ago. I've known so many shady characters in my lifetime that I was probably well acquainted with most of the other firebugs.

On January 13, 1932, at 2 a.m., McPeak's Shore Gardens, formerly the Villa Napoli, and before that the R.H. Stearns estate, was badly gutted by fire and had to be torn down.

Three men, who were fighting the fire, went into the large gambling room that was only slightly damaged. They opened a door into an adjacent bedroom. They pulled a large suitcase from under the bed. It was very heavy and when they opened it they found it full of wrapped rolls of quarters obviously for use in the slot machines. The three men split the contents of the suitcase. The fact that the money was not removed beforehand would make it seem that the fire was accidental rather than intentional.

All the other big hotels have long since been torn down. The Pacific House, Tivoli, Nantasket Hotel, Ocean View Hotel, Oregon House and Pemberton Hotel – all gone.

A former building commissioner of the town told me that his mother, when she first came here, stayed at the Pemberton Hotel. The rate for one room was $1,000 for the summer season. She told him of the 50,000-gallon steam-heated swimming pool fed with a constant flow of salt water pumped in from the ocean, located on the ground floor. The pool was always featured in the hotel's advertisements.

In the late '80's and '90's, through the turn of the century, well-to-do people came here and built expensive estates and spacious summer homes on Atlantic Hill, Green Hill, Bayside, Ocean Front, Allerton and Hull Hill. They all employed from two to six servants, owned fine horses and carriages, had coachmen and later chauffeurs. The town maintained three blacksmith shops and eight large livery stables. Although there were only a few families living here in the winter months, these facilities were set up to care for the needs of the wealthy summer residents. The townspeople were very receptive and did everything in their power to induce them to come here.

No one, living today, could look into Nantasket's authentic past without being thoroughly amazed at the enormous wealth of our summer population at the turn of the century. I have in my possession *The South Shore Blue Book of 1903*, compiled by Edward A. Jones, containing the lists of wealthy summer residents of the principal resorts along the South Shore from Nantasket all the way to Falmouth on Cape Cod, and one-third of the whole book is used to list the wealthy summer residents of Nantasket.

Floretta Vining, famous newspaperwoman of that time, was a unique character. She looked, dressed and acted like Queen Victoria. One of her closest friends was Hetty Greene, the richest woman in the world, who spent many of her summer vacations at Miss Vining's Stoney Beach Villa.

In compiling a book of this kind, it was necessary for many weeks to root through the archives of the State House in Boston and peruse the newspapers and periodicals of the eighties and nineties. Miss Vining's weekly newspapers, the *Hull Beacon* and the *Nantasket Breeze*, devoted a six-column page each week listing the arrivals of the wealthy visitors to the hotels and summer homes.

Reading through the Metropolitan newspapers and the social registers based on the estimated wealth of the summer residents, it was acknowledged by all that at the turn of the century, Nantasket was the richest summer resort on the entire Atlantic seaboard.

It was the most famous seashore resort in the United States and one of the most famous in the world. It's resplendent steamboat line to Boston, old Paragon Park as the East Coast's miniature world's fair, plush hotels and immense wealth – all that is long since gone and sighs won't bring it back.

In 1939 the old political machine, that had the town by the throat for forty-six years, was broken. Who broke it, is not important. That it was broken, is.

Now, our big problem is "Honkytonk." Everybody knows that. Each year our town gets worse.

We wait for some young, strong leader to solve the big one. He will have to rally the people around him because he will need the kind of help that Rudyard Kipling called "the everlasting teamwork of every bloomin' soul."

VIII

FORK IN THE ROAD

There were a few amusements on the area taken over from the town by the Metropolitan Park Commission in 1899, but they were short-lived as the State made it plain they were not in the amusement business.

In 1904, the Eastern Park Construction Company, owned by a group of Boston capitalists, was formed with the late George A. Dodge as manager. Plans were drawn up to construct a huge amusement park. But before the twenty-five acres of land were acquired, to be sure of no interference, the management saw to it that the political boss was provided with a substantial interest in the venture.

Old Nantasket had come to a fork in the road. Would it follow the quiet road to continued riches, or the noisy one to a honky-tonk community? The political boss, John Smith, stood like a stone statue at the fork, and a stern finger was pointed down the honky-tonk road; and by so doing, he threw the whole place wide open to amusements.

This was not an ordinary amusement park. It was like an exposition, a miniature world's fair. Smith and many others thought the park would maintain its original dignity and grandeur, as was attested by the following article written by the editor of the *Hull Beacon*, January 20, 1905:

"'Oh! I think I can see it all now: The flags flying, the building alive with lights and colors, the bands playing, the gondolas gliding silently along the canals. Oh! It's so vivid a picture. So entrancing.' These were the exclamations of delight I heard escape from the lips of a prominent Beacon Street matron who was in earnest conversation with Mr. Geo. A. Dodge as I entered his State Street office last Saturday.

"And indeed not only this Beacon Street individual, but hundreds of thousands of New Englanders will go into raptures before many months have passed, over the stupendous, bewildering creation that this same Geo. A. Dodge is constructing at Nantasket beach.

"Mr. Dodge can truthfully be called a modern captain of industry, for from chaos he built order, out of a barren unsightly waste of terra firma, a beautifully laid out World's Fair of amusements and pleasure gardens that will rank second to none when completed. And all this in a few weeks.

"But to dwell on the personality of this man of immense undertakings. A few years ago he was unheard of in the amusement world, although being popular and successful in commercial circles. Today his name is the Alpha and Omega of the summer amusement managers' conversation.

"Every concessionaire, every electrical engineer, every landscape gardener, every show manager in the country is acknowledging his prowess, his skill at organizing and directing a work which seems Herculean in its magnitude. And although having hundreds of callers daily, receiving letters by the thousand and dictating as many more, he is ever the same calm, quiet, self-possessed, and wears the kindly smile that is the secret of his successes. Never a caller but has seen him, no matter how trivial the mission.

"'With 25 acres of land, which includes the Rockland house property, I intend to give New Englanders a park that they will be proud of,' said Mr. Dodge. 'The nightly illumination will be a feature in itself, 100,000 electric lights will be installed, with an electric tower 150 feet high as the chief display. Twenty gigantic, as well up-to-date shows will encircle a fairy lagoon on which will ply gondolas. An open and free circus will be a constant feature, as well as excellent concert bands rendering music at every hour of the day and night. A Wild West show, trained animal show, flying machines, miniature railroad, earth's queer people, Canals of

SCHLITZ PALM GARDEN

Schlitz Palm Garden, Paragon Park. Rockland House in background, 1908.

(Courtesy R. Loren Graham)

PANORAMA VIEW OF PARAGON PARK, 1905

Taken from the upper veranda of the famous Schlitz Palm Garden.

(Courtesy Marie Willock)

Venice, costly mammoth ball room, riding elephants and camels and Japanese tea gardens will also be offered for the public's amusement.'

"Paragon Park will employ its own police force, some forty in number, to preserve order; also its own fire department.

"Conventions, picnic and excursion parties numbering up into the thousands can be readily taken care of daily without the least effort, for, together with the newly acquired Rockland house, the capacity will reach 100,000 a day.

"Mr. Dodge states the day of opening will be May 30th, and that the Park's completion will occur some two weeks previous to that date. 'These two weeks will be taken up in rehearsing the many attaches with their respective labors, so that when the public pour in through the gates all will be smooth and calm. No frustrated attendants, no mistakes.

"And we believe him, for the director is systematic, calm and self-possessed.

"Here's good luck to Geo. A. Dodge and to his undertaking."

With the fine character and magnitude of this venture it was highly possible that Smith and others may not have realized the seriousness of their mistaken judgment.

R. H. Stearns, of the Boston department store by the same name, built a beautiful estate adjacent to the Col. George F. Hall estate. Jacob P. Bates, of the Boston grocery firm of Cobb, Bates and Yerxa, built an elaborate mansion on Atlantic Hill only a stone's throw away. It was completed one year before Paragon Park was built. His heart was broken and all three men stated many times that they would never have built their estates here if they knew that an amusement park would be constructed two hundred yards away. Stearns and Bates lost all interest and disposed of their estates as best

JOHNSTOWN FLOOD, PARAGON PARK, 1906
(Courtesy Daniel A. Short)

BOARDWALK AND CASINO, NANTASKET BEACH, 1950
Southern end of the old Nantasket Hotel

they could and along with the other wealthy families in the area, moved away.

With the building of Paragon Park the exodus had started and in a few fleeting years, Nantasket and its summer million-aires came to a parting of the ways. It was very plain that parks and other amusements with their inevitable honkytonk environment did not then, and never will, attract the kind of people that build expensive summer homes.

The choice was caviar or hot dog, and the hot dog got the nod.

Nantasket's official name is Hull. Starting with May 29, 1644, when the town was incorporated and named Hull, history does not recall a speck of scandal in its local govern-ment. The officials were all upright, honest men and their old New England town meeting form of government up until 1893 was, as far as history records, as clean as the driven snow.

IX

BOSS SMITH

On March 6, 1893, John Smith was elected to the Hull Board of Selectmen. He was an imposing personality. His family name was Schmidt and had been changed to Smith. He was of Prussian ancestry. He had a commanding military bearing. He was a natural-born leader and just a look at him would tell that he belonged out front. He was always meticulous in his dress. He was punctual and exacting in everything he did. When Smith was elected in 1893, he became the boss of the most ruthless complete political domination of any community anywhere, anytime, under the Stars and Stripes. The political machine that he founded and bossed stood up for forty-six years and nobody in all that time was able to punch a pinhole in it. For the first twenty-six years of his reign it was an utter impossibility for anyone to even be nominated as a candidate against his slate of officers.

It's a good doctor who successfully treats a case of smallpox, but the one who concocts a vaccine that prevents the disease is a better one. A smart politician may be able to wiggle his way out of a jam, but it would be a smarter one who would have prevented the jam.

On the evening of October 8, 1871, a fire, generally acknowledged to have been caused when Mrs. O'Leary was milking her cow and the cow kicked the lantern over, broke out on the west side of the city and spread to the three divisions of Chicago, resulting in one of the most destructive conflagrations on record. A total of 18,000 buildings were destroyed and the loss was set at $187,000,000. John Smith and everyone else in the world knew that the Chicago fire would never have occurred if Mrs. O'Leary had placed the lantern where the cow couldn't kick it over.

Smith applied the principle of prevention to politics. To stop an unwanted event from happening was better than having to deal with it after it happened.

Boss Smith's Town Meeting

The Town of Hull, like all other small Massachusetts towns, operates under the old New England town meeting form of government. The registered voters of the town gathered once a year, usually in March, at the town hall.

The presiding officer, the Moderator, stands at a large table on the platform. The Town Clerk sits at the end of the table and records all that goes on during the meeting.

Each item to be acted on is called an Article, each Article is numbered and the total list of all the Articles is known as the Town Meeting Warrant. When the voting on all the articles is completed the meeting is adjourned and over.

Ever since the town was founded up to March 3, 1919, all the town officials were nominated from the floor and elected in the town meeting. It was just another article in the warrant. There was no such thing as an election day up to that time.

On June 26, 1907, a bill passed by the Massachusetts Legislature, Chapter 560, Section 392 of the Acts of 1907, to set up a separate day for towns to select their officials by the use of the official ballot as is done today. This bill was made law ninety days after its passage. It then became Section 6, Chapter 41 of the General Laws which reads as follows:

"A town may, at a town meeting, vote that official ballots as defined in section one, chapter fifty, shall thereafter be used therein; and may at the annual town meeting or at a meeting held at least thirty days before the annual town meeting, by a two-thirds vote, rescind such action. In town elections in which official ballots are used, nominations for

POLITICAL BOSS, JOHN SMITH
(Courtesy R. Oliver Olson)

town officers elected by ballot shall be made, ballots and other apparatus there-for provided, and elections of such officers conducted, in accordance with chapters fifty to fifty-six, inclusive, so far as applicable."

This was permissive legislation, that is, while it was a state law it did not become a town law till the voters, by majority vote at a town meeting, adopted its provisions.

While nearly all the towns adopted this law immediately after its enactment the Old Ring, as the political machine was called, blocked its adoption until March 4, 1918.

Since the law's passage, in 1907, repeated requests were made by citizens and citizen groups to have an article in the town meeting warrant accepting this law, but all were ignored by the Ring. Time after time, legal petitions with the required number of signatures were filed with the selectmen and they were either "mislaid," "some word misspelled," or they were not "filed on time." Finally, the members of the Old Ring started to break ranks. They thought Smith had gone too far. Dissension seemed on its way and after noisy demands, Boss Smith told his co-workers to put the damn thing in the town warrant. "We'll beat them anyway." So the article was finally inserted in the town meeting warrant of March 4, 1918.

It was the wildest town meeting ever held in any Massachusetts community. The meeting got completely out of control, the police were helpless, chairs and tables were toppled over, a half dozen fist fights broke out, the moderator's table was knocked over and the town clerk's records were strewn all over the place.

After the vote was all cast it began to quiet down. But when the tellers started to tabulate the votes, a mob gathered around them, and as the count was going on they demanded to see the yes and no vote slips and the confusion lasted more than two hours. After three recounts, the vote was finally announced: 162 in favor, 124 opposed. And after long last, the election day and its secret official ballot became a part of the Hull Town Government.

Smith was strong enough to take that chance, lose and not be hurt. His supporters never left him, they only openly differed with him on that one issue. It was the only reverse he ever experienced in his political career. He tried for the impossible, "to prevent people from voting." When Smith couldn't do it, no one could.

On March 28, 1902, the Citizens Association was formed in Hull: John Smith, President; James Jeffrey, First Vice-President; John L. Mitchell, Second Vice-President. The Executive Committee was John Smith, Alfred A. Galiano, James Jeffrey, Richard B. Hayes, Eugene Mitchell, Jr., John D. Coyle, Captain William Mitchell, George H. Hatchard and William Sherriff.

The association met once a year, just before the annual town meeting, and dues were set at one dollar a year. Most of the voters were members and that's where their influence ended. They were told at each annual meeting that if anyone did not support the association slate of candidates in its entirety, and their recommended action in the town meeting, he should leave the hall.

Lobster salad sandwiches and plenty of drinks were provided, but the only part the association members played in this amazing political drama was to sit, listen and obey. But at that they had it better than the citizens in the town meeting.

Who the slate of candidates would be, and what was going to happen in the town meeting, would all be cut and dried in a meeting of a handful of Smith's lieutenants in a smoke-filled hotel room two weeks before the Citizens Association Meeting.

Boss Smith would brook no interference with what he set out to do. From the beginning of his reign, he always announced a month in advance of the town meeting exactly what the tax rate would be. He told the heads of the town departments who made up Smith's advisory board, after getting advance figures of outside assessments levied against the town, to bring in their total estimated operating cost to fit into the tax rate that he had previously announced. The tax rate was always exactly as he said it would be.

For the first twenty-six of the forty-six years of complete domination by the old political ring there were no election days. All the town officials were chosen in the town meeting.

The big boss, John Smith, always sat with his back against the side wall so he could see the Moderator and everyone else in the hall. The meeting was opened with a prayer for divine guidance by a local clergyman. With the closing words of the reverend gentleman all religious scruples went out the window.

One of the first matters to be acted on was the election of the town officials and this is the way the ring operated. The friendly Moderator knew exactly who to recognize so when the right man stood up to address the chair he was given the floor and would read the following motion, all typed out for him beforehand: "I nominate John Smith for selectman and move the nominations be closed." The Moderator would then say, "All those in favor of John Smith for selectman say 'aye'." "I declare Smith duly elected." There was no sense in asking for the "no" votes, because there was no other candidate to vote for.

Every once in a while some foolish man would jump up and address the Moderator to nominate someone else and as he did some stooge would address the Moderator and rise to a point of order. He would mumble some senseless remarks that no one could hear. The Moderator would state that the point of order was well taken and order the foolish man to "sit down, you're out of order." If he stood up again the

Moderator would direct the police to throw him out of the hall for "disturbing the meeting."

In the March, 1904, town meeting a citizen coughed and sneezed at the same time. They threw him out of the hall. They thought he said something.

In those days the Moderator was the absolute boss of the town meeting. His decisions were final. But the decisions he made were not his. Every move the Moderator made was dictated to him by John Smith, the Old Ring boss. If he failed to carry out every detail of Smith's instructions he would be severely dealt with and he knew it. To doubt the vote or appeal from the decision of the Moderator was unheard of in Smith's day. Any such motion would be completely ignored.

In 1904, some smart aleck brought a ruling down from the State House that it was illegal to nominate a candidate for town office and at the same time move that the nominations be closed, so all the voter could do was nominate the candidate and someone else had to move the nominations be closed.

The answer to that was to have two of the Ring members jump up at the same time. The act was very carefully rehearsed and the Moderator selected the right man to make the nomination, and as they stood up so close together he would assign the floor to the other to move the nominations be closed.

This went along, town meeting after town meeting, without interference from anyone. Smith never spoke in a town meeting, and he was once asked why. He said, "I can't think with my mouth open." For twenty-six years it was made impossible to have a candidate against anyone of Smith's slate of town officers, and during all that time every article in every town meeting went exactly as he directed. For those twenty-six years it was the most complete political domination of any community under the American flag. John Smith ruled his bailiwick exactly one hundred percent, and if my arithmetic is correct that's as far as you can go.

All the Citizens Association accomplished was to give the Old Ring corrupt political machine a respectable name.

X

THE CLOSED CORPORATION

Boston's Martin Lomasney, one of the better-known old time big city bosses, operated through his Hendricks Club in old Ward Eight of the West End. He was the old master of Boston politics for over thirty years. Every office seeker knew full well that his chances were poor if he did not have the blessing of the Irish politician who taught snooty Boston the ABC's of roughneck politics.

Smith and Lomasney met and became good friends. Smith invited him to Hull. He sat on the platform as a guest at the March town meeting of 1915, and watched this small town political machine in action. They flew through the town meeting like a machine gun. The election of town officers and the business of the meeting was completed in eighteen minutes. The average town meeting in any other community would last from three to five hours.

Later on, Lomasney invited Smith to a pre-election meeting of his Hendricks Club in Boston's West End. Smith sat on the platform as a guest, as Lomasney did in Hull. It must be kept in mind that Lomasney, the big city political boss, operated under the city charter form of government – Smith under the New England town meeting form.

Lomasney's influence in Boston and throughout Massachusetts was vast. Smith's influence in the little town was small. But in presenting his guest to the Hendricks Club members, Lomasney openly admitted from the platform that as far as the complete domination of the electorate was concerned, Smith had it over him like a circus tent. Lomasney had to get his candidates elected, Smith did not. The citizens had to vote for those on Smith's slate or not vote at all. There was just no one else to vote for.

For twenty-six years, from 1893 to 1919, there were no town election days. For the next twenty years, there were annual town election days. Even with candidates against them each year, the efforts to gain any headway against the Old Ring were woefully weak. And so, for forty-six years, the people of Hull had absolutely nothing to say about their own government.

The Old Ring could support a wild baboon in a cage against a clergyman of the Gospel and the gentleman of the cloth would surely go down to ignominious defeat. The only way a citizen could live in peace and happiness was to keep his nose clean, his mouth shut and do as he was told.

I remember one year, the Old Ring sensed some opposition to an article in the town meeting warrant. The members of the Citizens Association (a fancy name for the Old Ring) lined up outside the hall and filed in. When the last member was admitted one of the members, William Reddie, put a big padlock on the door. I was a member in good standing of the Old Ring at the time. I came there late and Reddie unlocked the door and let me in, then locked it up again leaving the other citizens of the town out in the cold and rain. They ran through the meeting in a hurry. The door was then opened and the other townspeople were invited in for coffee and sandwiches. From there on Reddie was known for the rest of his life as "Padlock Bill" Reddie.

The domination by the big boss and his Old Ring extended far beyond political boundaries. They regulated, to an alarming degree, the daily lives of the people. All the business establishments in the town were owned by members of the Old Ring. The big boss, Smith, owned the Nantasket Ice Company. No one else was allowed to peddle ice in Hull. The police saw to that. In those days ice was the only method of refrigeration. The people either bought their ice from Smith or went without it.

The Chief of Police owned the Nantasket Coal Company.

Every citizen in Hull knew that it was suicidal to buy coal from any other dealer. My brother had his dental office in the adjacent town of Cohasset. He and a partner bought the building. At first they were operating on a shoestring and the Cohasset coal dealer was kind enough to give the coal to heat the place and wait till the following summer for his money. The coal dealer's family and friends were very helpful to my brother in getting started in his profession. So they asked if they could deliver a couple of tons of coal to our home in Hull. The only thing my brother could say was "yes." So when they delivered the coal, the Old Ring snoopers spotted them putting it in our cellar. On the following evening when we had finished dinner, we were visited by three members of the Old Ring. Our family was all together that evening and they gave us an unmerciful raking over the coals. And as they left, we were told in no uncertain terms that it was never to happen again.

We all kept quiet during the bawling out. My father was big and strong enough to throw the three of them out of the house, but he did not want the axe to fall on the rest of his family. This was not an isolated incident. It happened to a greater or lesser degree at some time or other to most of the families of Hull. The crime of buying coal from any other company was not easily forgiven.

On April 4, 1913, the Old Colony Gas Company was granted a franchise to bring gas into the bordering town of Hingham and the following year, 1914, the installation was completed. An application was made at the same time to have the gas lines come into Hull. Permission was refused. The old political ring blocked the gas company from coming into the town of Hull for sixteen years. A franchise was finally granted July 21, 1929, and the following year, 1930, gas was installed throughout the town. Up to that time, you burned their coal in your home or you burned nothing.

The local insurance company was owned by the tax

collector who was also a selectman. Two grocery stores were owned by Old Ring members and while they did not tell the citizen where to buy his food, he knew his environment and could sense in the air what they wanted him to do. He bought their groceries in his caution not to aggravate them.

The one automobile agency in the town was owned by a top official of the Old Ring. No town employee and very few others dared to buy a car from any outside dealer. He held the Studebaker agency. I, and about everyone else drove Studebaker cars as long as he held the agency. If a car buyer got behind in his notes he would be given a town job. The town treasurer would then deduct the amount of the car notes for the dealer. The town employee would get a pay check for what was left. The employee had no Civil Service or any other protection. As soon as his notes were all paid he would be dropped and another debtor appointed in his place.

The best way to get appointed to the Police or Fire Department was to run up a bill on any of the companies owned by the members of the Old Ring. One man I knew, who got in debt to the coal company, made his police job last longer than the others. Each time the town treasurer took a coal payment from his paycheck he charged more coal and had it delivered to his home. This went on for quite a while. He knew he would hold his job as long as he owed money for the coal. They stopped delivering coal to his house and when his coal account was paid they fired him. They wanted his job so they could get a rope around some of the other debtors. He did not do too bad. He wound up with a heap of coal in his backyard that lasted him for the next three years.

The call firemen were paid two hundred dollars per year. They were paid each year just before Christmas. When the town treasurer got through taking out what they owed there was very little left. It worked something like the company store at the coal mines. That was the origin of the boomerang dollar. It went out from the town treasury, cut a circle, and came back into the pockets of the members of the Old Ring. The citizen of today might ask, "Weren't they afraid of losing these people's votes?" They had no voting privileges. They were scared to death.

Family after family left the church they were brought up in and attended the church the Old Ring went to. You could tell who they were. When the influence of the Old Ring waned they came back to their own church. It was generally known that a prominent carpenter here in Hull sought and obtained permission from the political boss to join the Holy Name Society.

The Old Ring was all Republican and I remember that for years there were only two registered Democrats in Hull. As late as 1928, when Al Smith ran for the Presidency, there were only six, yet that year he carried the town.

The Old Ring was capable of meting out punishment to "wrong doers." Many an otherwise respectable citizen, for his unfriendly remarks about the machine, wound up doing a hitch in the county jail.

In 1911, a foolhardy newspaperman set out in a series of articles to expose some of the scurrilous goings-on in the town government. His first article appeared in the morning edition of a Boston newspaper and on that very night his house here mysteriously broke out in fire. The response of the Nantasket authorities was equally mysterious. Orders were given that under no circumstances could a fireman or a piece of equipment leave the station only three hundred feet away, until the last wisp of smoke slowly curled away in the night air.

John F. Fitzgerald, the renowned ancestor of the Presidential Kennedys, attended a town meeting some years ago and asked permission to address the gathering. He was at first refused but on reconsideration, he was allowed to talk. He stood up and blasted hell out of the town officials and their political machine. Lo and behold, the next day a ditch was dug, five feet wide and seven feet deep, in front of his summer home and it remained there all summer in spite of the mayor's vigorous attempts to get it filled in. The town finally did close the abyss, but not until the summer season had closed first and his summer house was abandoned.

Everyone knew that if he didn't "behave himself" the bad end of the stick would be waiting for him.

XI

CONTROLLED ELECTIONS

I joined the Citizens Association (the Old Ring) in 1915, but it was not until 1921 that I was asked to take part in the funny business of controlled elections. On election day, the employees of each town department and their families were lined up in a solid block to cast their votes. For example, the highway department and families had to report to the polling place at a given time. They were lined up in a single file. No one else was allowed in line. The police officer would hold the line back until all the voters in the enclosure had voted and gone out.

As the voter entered the polling enclosure his name was checked off, he was given an official ballot, he then went into a stall and marked his ballot. From there he walked over and put his ballot in the slot provided in the ballot box and his name was checked on his way out.

When the ballot was inserted in the box the operator turned a crank on the side of the box. The ballot was drawn in, marked with a cancellation stamp, then turned nose down, came upside down in the opposite direction, slid off the metal apron and fell face down in the bottom of the box. Each successive ballot would fall on top of the one before. If two or three hundred ballots were left in the ballot box, the pile might get too tall and some ballots slide off the top. That would stop the continuity and, of course, spoil the Old Ring's game. If one hundred or one hundred and fifty votes were cast before removing them from the ballot box there would be little or no chance of them not being in sequence. There is probably no one who had had a more thorough schooling in the operation of the ballot box than I have. I was very well trained in that respect by the Old Ring. I participated in their controlled elections.

I went over the ballot box operation with three different experienced town clerks and I spent one entire afternoon with the ballot box open, sliding through facsimile ballots the same size and folded like the official ballot, with the present Hull town clerk, John F. Darcy, and they were all in agreement with me that, if there were only fifty ballots cast and then removed from the box, as the Old Ring used to do, it would be utterly impossible for them to fall in any other way than the order in which they were put in the ballot box. That voting box is a machine and each ballot falls in exactly the same place on the floor of the box. If a voter was the thirty-fifth to put his ballot in the box, his would be the thirty-fifth from the bottom or the sixteenth from the top, in the block of fifty.

Everyone employed in the voting enclosure – Moderator, Town Clerk, operator of the ballot box, police officer who had the key and removed the ballots from the box, tellers, checkers and all were loyal workers for the Old Ring.

Permission was, of course, given by the Moderator and Town Clerk to remove the ballots from the ballot box in blocks of fifty. When the first fifty ballots were put in the box everything was held up. The policeman would then unlock the box, tuck the ballots in neatly, and then place the pile of fifty at a certain place on the table nearby, exactly as they were piled in the box. Then the voting was allowed to continue until the next fifty had voted. The voting was again stopped while the police officer opened the box and removed the next block of fifty and carefully placed them on the table in the order in which they were stacked in the box. Each block of fifty was taken out in the same careful manner until the polls were closed. The police officer and those who tabulated the ballots were very carefully trained – after each fifty were taken and counted they were put in an envelope in exactly the same order in which they were taken from the box. Each envelope was numbered 1, 2, 3 and so forth.

My job was to sit at a table outside the rail where the voter was checked off and given his ballot. I wrote down the name of each voter that was given a ballot and I wrote down the number after his name in the order in which he put his ballot in the box, number one would be marked after his name, the second voter would be number two, and so on.

The ballot box was placed much closer to the rail than it is today and twisted so I could see the indicator very plainly. No one was permitted to block my view. The checkers worked slowly so as to give me enough time to write the name of the voter down and the number that registered when he put his ballot in the box. When the police officer took out a block of fifty and before the tellers started to count I would send the list of fifty voters and the number after each name into the counting table so the tellers could see how each voted. The tellers made up their own list of the ones who voted "wrong."

If the number after a voter's name was 420, that meant that his ballot was the twentieth ballot from the bottom in the number 9 envelope that contained the ninth block of fifty. The leaders of the Old Ring knew how everybody voted. They took their time about sealing the envelopes and putting them away in a large box so they had plenty of time to find out all they wanted to know. My father called me a whippersnapper when I came home and told him how he voted.

The Old Ring's game could never have worked if the designer of the ballot box had the floor slanted so the ballot would drop and slide over to the other side, or if a rung was placed across the inside of the box so the ballot would drop on it and tumble to the floor. If these conditions did exist I imagine that the Old Ring would have a carpenter level the floor or take out the rung.

The secret ballot was not much of a secret to the Old Ring.

One election day, some ward heeler in the Roxbury section of Boston scooped up a bus load of men from the street corners and barrooms and sent then down to Hull. A member of the Old Ring was on the bus and handed out slips of paper showing them who to vote for. They were given a feed and a few drinks at a local hotel. None of them were on the Hull voting list and most of them had never been in the town before. It is my recollection that there were twenty-eight in the group. As they came in to vote they were lined up in a single file. They were held back until all the voters in the enclosure had gone out. Each of the twenty-eight walked past the checkers and were handed a ballot. All the checkers and I did was to count the number of "voters" that went through. The same happened at the exit check table.

Right after the polls were closed the incoming and outgoing checklists were brought together and twenty-eight voters who had not voted were checked off on each list as having voted. It was always a good showing when eighty percent of the registered voters turned out. So there were always plenty of voters who had not voted that could be checked off.

In this particular election an old lady who had passed away at four o'clock in the morning was checked off as having voted when the polls did not open until four hours after she died.

I acted in the same capacity at the Hull town elections of 1922 through 1926, and I was told by officials of the Old Ring that the same thing happened in 1920. In 1927, Stevens discontinued the snooping operation. But the notion persisted with most of the voting public for several years afterwards that the Old Ring knew how everyone voted. To have people in that frame of mind was just as effective for the Old Ring as if they knew how everyone voted.

The Old Ring workers showed me how they steamed the

glue off the envelopes of absentee and shut-in ballots. The absentee ballot envelopes are of manila paper and if steamed carefully, using a penknife to lift the flap, can be opened and with a little glue brush, can be sealed back just as they were before. With a manila envelope it worked best from the edge of the flap back.

If, having opened an absentee ballot, we found the voter voting wrong, we would "correct his mistake." If the ballot was marked with a pencil we merely erased his crosses and put down the correct ones. If the ballot was marked in ink, we had a special ink eradicator and a special white blotter so we could make the ballot look as if there was never a mark on it. The Old Ring workers told me where to buy it. Of course we'd make the "corrections" on that one too.

While it was the rottenest of rotten politics, it was amusing indeed to find someone who had pledged his undying loyalty, signed our nomination papers and prayed for our success, and then to steam open his ballot and find him voting for the opposition right from top to bottom.

A lady who was after us to put her son on the Police Department became sick and had to vote by absentee ballot. We steamed her ballot open and found she had voted against us. She wondered why her son never got the job.

On March 3rd, 1919, in order to put a sanctimonious frosting on their political shenanigans, the Old Ring nominated and elected as town moderator, the Reverend Frank Kingdon, minister of the Hull Methodist Episcopal church. The poor man was new to the town and did not know what he was in for. Up on the platform it was plain that he was a fish out of water. When he saw what was going on, there was some speculation that he might not finish the meeting but he stuck it out. It was damn plain that they would never get him back there again and they never did.

Smith's machine was so perfectly set up that he had carefully groomed Henry J. Stevens, his fellow selectman and

Chief of the Fire Department, as his successor and kept him at his side constantly. He trained him in his method of operation so that when Smith died on July 28, 1926, and the baton was passed, the transition was so smooth that his political machine was just the same as if he was still there and ruling the roost. Stevens took up where Smith left off. Some of us thought, now that Smith was gone, there might be a chance to break up the Old Ring.

At a meeting of the Citizens Association in 1928, the President of the Association said, "Anyone who does not want to go along with what the Association wanted must leave the hall," so five of us got up and walked out. That was the beginning of the fireworks. We all realized that we were pawns in their organization.

They took quite a chunk of land from me in the widening of Rockland House Road. Under the law they were obliged to pay for the land they took. I would have been satisfied if they had given a small token payment that would have denoted friendliness, but they kidded the pants off me and I wound up with nothing. The others, who walked out with me, had similar experiences.

Shortly afterwards, I attended a christening in the town and had a heavy feed of Italian wine. On my way driving home, I plowed into another car. A fireman, who was also a special police officer, was the first on the scene. He put me in his car and took me to the home of one my friends. The fireman told the regular police officer, who was sent to investigate, that I was sober and that's the way the report was made out on the local insurance office typewriter. In this report the police officer got a piece of carbon paper twisted in the machine. A lady friend of mine working in the insurance office found the carbon paper that the police officer left behind on which his complete report was printed on the back side. She gave the carbon paper to me. The report stated that I was sober.

The police were sent to my home, but there was nobody

there. They couldn't find me and so there was no way of their knowing whether I was drunk or sober.

When the police officer turned in his report, the Chief of Police told him to make out a second report stating that I was drunk. The next morning I was served with a summons to appear in the District Court to answer to a charge of drunken driving. My brother was a Hull police officer, and to rub it in good, they had him serve the summons on me. The first and second reports were worded exactly the same with the exception that the word "sober" in the first report was changed to the word "drunk" in the second one.

When the case came up in the District Court, the police officer presented the second report. I told the judge that the original report had been changed and I threw the original report, on the back of the carbon paper, on the judge's desk. I was found "not guilty." The truth of the matter is that on the night of the accident I was so drunk I couldn't hit the ground with my hat.

On Thanksgiving Day, 1929, when the steamboats burned, I was arrested again for drunken driving. This time they put me in the lockup. The next morning they took me to the Hingham District Court in the next town. While the customary fine for offenses like mine was twenty-five dollars, the judge sandbagged me one hundred and twenty-five dollars. I had no money in my pocket, but I had sold a piece of property the day before and had a five thousand dollar certified check in my pocket. I asked the court clerk if I could go to the bank and cash it, but they put handcuffs on me. They wouldn't let me have my hat. Two police officers led me across the main square of the town, where I graduated from High School, to the bank. I had then been a practising dentist for fifteen years. The same parade crossed the square back to the courthouse where I paid the fine.

As was proven later, those episodes did not hurt me politically because most of my constituents took a little something for medicinal purposes.

XII

VOTING INVESTIGATION

In March, 1932, inspectors were sent down from the Elections Division of the Secretary of State's Office to conduct a voting investigation at the request of our opposition group. They kept a very sharp check on the town election procedure. The Old Ring was on its good behavior while the state inspectors were breathing down their necks and nothing wrong was found.

The investigation of the Hull voting list that followed was something else again. The state inspection team went over the list with a fine tooth comb. They found sixteen men registered on the voting list who were also registered on the voting lists of three other communities where they operated a big dice game. They moved the game from one community to another and in addition to paying the officials in each place, it was to their further advantage to have a voting block in each of the four locations.

A Hull man owned a home on Atherton Road. He also owned the next vacant lot on which he had installed a cesspool. Four men were registered from the vacant lot. It was probably the only time in the history of Massachusetts that four voters were registered from a cesspool.

In another instance a man was registered from a vacant lot that had a large a tree in the center. We spent three days trying to find the man for questioning, but no one knew where he was. One of the inspectors suggested that he might be found sitting on the top of a hurdy-gurdy. Another gave the public library as his voting residence.

When the voting census was taken, it was not uncommon for them to call on an old lady, living alone in her home, to question her about two or three others registered from the same address, of whom she had never heard in her life.

There were a good many mattress voters, some legitimate and some not. Some were registered to vote who didn't know a letter in the alphabet. One time, a man bought an old house that had an outhouse behind it. He moved the house to another location but left the outhouse there. Sometime after that, three people registered from the otherwise vacant lot. Near the close of the next election the three people had not voted and a campaign worker for the Old Ring was sent over to see if the three voters were in the outhouse. He reported back that there was nobody home.

In 1932, I was put up as a candidate for the Town Moderator and I was defeated by only sixty votes, 622 to 682. I seemed to be able to get more votes than anyone in our group. Some thought it was because so many had come to my dental office, although it was hard to understand how a dentist's patients could be as fond of him as that. I used to think it was because I was so tall and handsome, at least that's what the ladies used to tell me.

I was a candidate for Moderator in 1933, and was defeated by 187 votes, and in 1937, I was defeated by a still worse margin of 216 votes. We had lost a lot of ground because so many legitimate voters were dragged up before the investigators and were embarrassed and humiliated that it seemed our cause was hopeless.

The voting investigation backfired and we were at a loss to know what to do. It was at this time that we became aware of our own shortcomings and political weaknesses. We had to get the advice and counsel of someone who knew more than we did. I had the good fortune to have hit up a friendship with the former Mayor of Boston, former Congressman, and former Governor of Massachusetts, James M. Curley, in the years that he was a summer resident here in Hull.

Three of us made an appointment with him in his Boston

home. He received us very cordially and sat down with us at a large table. He knew the town pretty well, he knew the officials and knew how the Old Ring operated. He went all over the groundwork with us. Curley told us that every political organization, big or small, has dissension in its ranks. He told us it was our job to find out where it was, then pour gasoline on it.

He asked us about the employment conditions in the town. We told him there was no employment – you couldn't buy a job and the town employees' pay was skimpy. He told us that, when we were ready to make the lunge, to go out and screech our heads off for the working man and his family. "Do what you possibly can to help them, but promise them anything."

With Curley's advice, we organized our forces and awaited developments. While Stevens was the big boss, unlike Smith, he neglected to train and groom his successor, and so at his untimely death in September, 1938, the leadership was "up for grabs."

Clarence V. Nickerson, schoolteacher, school principal, superintendent of schools, Town Treasurer, Chairman of Selectmen and President of the Hull Citizens Association (the Old Ring) moved out front.

John R. Wheeler, the local automobile dealer, next to Stevens, was the most powerful figure in the Old Ring. He was the money man in the background. He was never out in front. He held several small elective and appointive offices. Wheeler and Stevens worked very closely together, and during the twelve years that Stevens was up front, the real boss was Wheeler. We all knew if Nickerson got the upper hand, Wheeler's power was gone. That was the opening that Curley told us to look for.

Three of our group made an appointment with Wheeler at his home. We had a very pleasant meeting. He told us he was thinking the same way we were. He had a solid block of voters in his own right. I was the spokesman for our side. I told Mr. Wheeler that our group wanted me to run for Selectman. I said that we knew we could not win unless his followers and ours were brought together. We gave Wheeler our word of honor if we were elected to the Board of Selectmen we would go along with him as the boss of the town. When we left Wheeler's home that night we all shook hands, our forces were joined and the campaign was on.

We then went to Boston to get further advice and guidance from Curley. After talking over the best way to get our message to the greatest number of voters, it was decided to broadcast our cause over a Boston Radio Station and make the whole speech about the working man and his family. He told us to talk about nothing else. I typed up a speech as he told us to, and brought the copy back for his O.K. He made a few corrections in it and said it was all right.

After notifying every voter in Hull by postal card a week in advance, I made the following spiel over Boston Radio Station WEEI on Friday, March 3rd, 1939 at 6:45 p.m.

"My fellow citizens of Hull:

"The use of the radio, my good friends, is about the only way I could think of to talk to all of the people of Hull at the same time and so, rather than ask you to attend meetings with uncertain weather conditions and so much sickness around, I thought it would be better to talk to you in the comfortable surroundings of your own homes.

"As you all know, I am a candidate for Selectman, not for the glory that might come to me, but because of the disgraceful treatment accorded the working people of Hull in the last thirteen years and particularly in the year just ended.

"Most of you remember when Selectman John Smith was Superintendent of Streets. New roads were built, sidewalks were constructed, there was a good deal of work on the highway department; the pay was $5.60 a day. The men worked six days a week, quitting Saturday at 11 o'clock with a full day's pay. Their weekly pay envelope contained $33.60. John Smith, the Lord rest his soul, never reduced a laborer's pay one five-cent piece. He passed away in July, 1926, and the years that have followed have shown everyone of us that the working people of Hull lost the best friend they ever had.

"Not long after his passing, the town officials reduced the laborer's pay to $5.00 a day, less work was done and fewer men employed and right in the middle of the depression, with still less work in sight, they further reduced the laborer's pay to $4.00 a day, the lowest wage, at that time, paid by any city or town in the entire Commonwealth.

"A movement was then started to increase the wages, and after a discussion in the town meeting of 1935, the wages were increased to $5.00 a day, with still less work and fewer men employed. In the town meeting of March, 1938, I made a motion to restore the pay of the laborers of Hull to its original wage scale of $5.60 a day. The motion was passed, and the then Commissioner of Public Safety, Henry J. Stevens, the Lord rest his soul, made a motion to increase the Highway appropriation $2500 so that no laborer would lose as much as one day's work by the increase and that their pay would be $33.60 a week. The motion to fix the daily wage at $5.60 a day passed. The motion to retain the six-day week at $33.60 passed. That was the clear mandate of the citizens of Hull to their duly elected public servants.

"Strange as it may seem, that was the end of the six day week in Hull. The five-day week was inaugurated for the Spring street cleaning. The weekly pay envelope was reduced to $28.00, in direct contradiction to the expressed will of a majority of the people.

"The only other work undertaken by the town all last year was the removal of the tracks of the New Haven Railroad bed. The three day week was then inaugurated, and the weekly pay envelope reduced to $16.80, just one-half of what was voted in the town meeting as the plain mandate of the people of Hull to their duly elected public servants.

"Now compare the working conditions of 13 years ago under John Smith with the working conditions of today. Thirteen years ago the working man of Hull was paid $5.60 a day. He worked six days each week, quitting Saturday at 11 o'clock with a full day's pay. He washed up, changed his clothes, sat down to his Saturday dinner with his family, his week's work done and $33.60 laying on the corner of the kitchen table. He was happy and contented, head of a respectable family. I know that, because my own father was one of them.

"Today, there is no work, able bodied citizens are walking the streets, day after day, week after week, in misery and despair, searching for work and can't find any. When they do get a week's work, which is not very often, their weekly pay envelope contains $16.80.

"In those thirteen years, in almost every instance, the salaries of the officials have been increased, while the working people were cut to the bone. There was not one cent's reduction in any official's salary in all those years. There is a concrete, firsthand example of wealth in the hands of a few with the resultant poverty and misery to the masses of our people.

"When there is no industry or other means of employment in a community, it then falls on the Government of that community to provide work for idle hands. There is no means of employment in Hull except for the influx of summer visitors and for the remaining nine months of the year our town, from an employment standpoint, is just a hell on earth.

"I am going to introduce a measure in the town meeting of March 11, to put 100 men to work for six months of the year at $5.60 with a six day week a half day Saturday with a full day's pay, making $33.60 a week.

"During the months of June, July, August and September, when the summer people are here, there is plenty of work for all. During January and February, very little outside work can be done, so that the six months would consist of the three fall months of October, November and December, and the three spring months of March, April and May.

"In addition to the $45,000 appropriated each year for the Highway Department, there could be a saving of at least $20,000 in the Public Welfare Department when the men are working. This $20,000 could be taken from the Public Welfare Department and added to the $45,000 Highway appropriation, making $65,000 available. It will require $100,000 to put these 100 men to work six months of the year, so $35,000 more will have to be raised, and I know, as most of you do, that $35,000 can be made by cutting down the crazy expenditures in other departments, without reducing any man's pay or the number of men employed, and so this plan can be put into operation, with no additional burden to the taxpayer whatever.

"Every once in a while, we read in the daily newspapers of some old recluse starving to death in an attic room with no heat, living in squalor and dirt. On complaint of neighbors, the police come, take him to a hospital and try to bring him back to life. They return, search the room, and find $20,000 or $40,000 under the mattress.

"Each year about January 1st, the local newspaper carries a big story of how the town of Hull is in as good financial condition as any town in the state, but they don't tell about the citizens of Hull walking the streets looking for work.

"I learned through hard knocks early in life, the value of genuine economy. I could never subscribe to that economy practiced by the starving recluse in the attic room. I could never subscribe to that economy practiced by the officials of

Hull, with a town treasury as good as any in the state and the people walking the streets in a hopeless search for work.

"Now, let's be frank. Taxes are paid into the town treasury to be used to bring the greatest benefit to all of the people. It was not the intention of the founding fathers or of their successors that the government of any community was formed to bring wealth and luxury to one or two men at the top and leave the rank and file of the people in poverty and want. That was not the Democracy that I learned in the history books in school, and I am sure with your help in the voting booth on March the 6th, that it is not the kind of Democracy that you and I are going to live under in the years to come.

"These young men, anxious for a start in life and the older men, heads of families, are our townspeople. They are the life blood of our community and we should do everything in our power to help these citizens whose futures are blackened by those shadows of adversity that from time to time fall across the lives of us all.

"As a boy I delivered groceries into the homes of most of the old families of Hull, I have had the happy privilege to have grown up among you and your old-fashioned honest ways, and now I lay my fate in the hands of you who know me best, confident that after all is said and done, I will be drawn a little closer to your hearts."

The Hull election of Monday, March 6th, marked the first time in forty-six years that anyone was elected to any office against the Old Ring; Edward J. Haley, our present town moderator, was elected to the Board of Assessors and I was elected to the Board of Selectmen.

We have always been willing to admit that it was not our own doing but the advice and guidance of James M. Curley who laid the groundwork for our initial success.

Curley had an extremely fascinating personality. He was very loyal to his friends and rough with his enemies.

James McNamara was, for several years, first mate for the Nantasket Steamboat Company. Many of the first mates who followed McNamara were appointed captains over his head and it was happening with such monotonous regularity that he felt he was being unfairly dealt with.

I asked him if he'd like to take the matter up with Curley. He said that it would do him no harm. I told Curley about his case. An appointment was made and the three of us met at Curley's home. To get the whole story straight he questioned McNamara for all of the details.

When he got through he picked up the telephone and called the manager of the Steamboat Company and the following day McNamara was notified of his appointment. He often said that if it wasn't for Curley's help he'd have stayed a first mate the rest of his life.

A great many people said rude things about Jim Curley. It must have been because they did not know him. I'm sure if they had got to know the magnificent old rogue they would never have said the things they did.

I always admired Curley in spite of the fact that, in 1935 while he was governor, I heaved his framed picture down the cellar stairs when he offered me the dental job at the Danvers Insane Asylum. I was very careful to see that he never found that out.

To have been elected one of three selectmen was to just get a "foot in the door." It was seven years later that we got control of the town government. We had several obligations to John R. Wheeler for his loyalty to us.

After the steamboat fire of 1929, the Nantasket Steamboat Company, faced with a constant passenger decline, was preparing to discontinue the service.

The Old Ring officials, realizing what would happen to Nantasket if there were no boat service, formed a company, bought the Nantasket Beach Steamboat Company, boats, wharfs, equipment and real estate in an effort to keep the boat service going between Nantasket and Boston.

After three disappointing summers of operating the line the new owners found that they had a white elephant on their hands.

The new company decided to try to sell the steamboat properties to the town of Hull.

Wheeler was the front man in the venture and our group backed him up. He got the necessary permission from the Massachusetts Legislature for the town to buy the boat property. It was known as Chapter 79 of the Acts of 1941, entitled "An Act Authorizing the Town of Hull to acquire Lands for Wharf and Recreation Center Purposes in Said Town" and appropriate a sum not to exceed $130,000 for the purpose and an article was inserted in the warrant of the Hull Town Meeting of March, 1941.

The property was spread around in so many different parcels that it took half the afternoon to read the motion that covered a dozen pages in the town report. The town voted to buy the property.

The whole business was dumped on the town and the owners were out from under.

That was over a quarter of a century ago and while the property was bought for recreation purposes not one square inch was ever used for recreation and probably never will be.

There were several other smaller obligations that Wheeler wanted from us and we stood by him and helped him all we could. In March, 1942, he was defeated for the Board of Health by Charles R. McCarthy, who later was elected to the Board of Selectmen, and from then on Wheeler's power faded out and he no longer took an active part.

XIII

ANOTHER SHADY DEAL

Before one town election, a friend and I went to the printing plant where the official ballots were being prepared. We told the manager we came to "inspect" the ballots to see if they were properly made out. When we got the manager's back turned I grabbed six ballots and put them in my overcoat pocket and brought them home with us. On election day we had three men stationed in a car across the street from the Municipal Building, they were provided with $100 in one dollar bills. We gave them the six ballots all marked with crosses after the names of our candidates. We had other workers at the entrance to the polling place watching out for those who might be interested in the price of a pint. When asked if they would take two dollars for their vote most all of them said, "yes." They thought that we would give them the two dollars and they could go upstairs and do as they pleased but it was not as easy as that. The voter was directed to report to the car across the street. He was given one of the ballots all marked. He was instructed to put this marked ballot in the ballot box and bring back the unmarked ballot that was given to him when he went in to vote, bring it back to the car and collect his two dollars. We had a trailer right behind him all the way so there would be no funny business.

After thirty-eight had gone through in this manner at a cost of seventy-six dollars some people began to get suspicious and we stopped it right there.

While I engineered this whole scheme, I kept aloof and appeared to have nothing to do with it. To gloss the thing over, I went before the friendly Board of Registrars of Voters and made a big stink. I told them I thought there was something fishy going on. Of course they laughed at me.

There may have been four or five who might have voted for us anyway but we knew that all thirty-eight were our votes.

We won that election by a rather small margin. People as old as I am are prone to lapses of memory. The date of that election, the candidates and the results? It seems one of those lapses of memory fits in here very nicely.

I was trained in the Old Ring rootin-tootin' school of slambang politics. The leaders of the old political machine were as honorable a group of men as could be found anywhere, but when it came to ruling their community they stopped at nothing and resorted to every dirty trick under the sun to win the town elections. I tried hard to be as honorable as they were but in politics I carried on the principles that they laid down.

It is pretty generally accepted that all of us come into this world in a state of mortal sin. We have a little larceny in our souls. Some wear their dishonesty on their sleeves and make no effort to hide it. With others, their dishonesty is confined to when no one is looking.

You who are reading this book are not more honest than I am merely because you conceal your dishonesty and I blather mine to the world.

The Old Ring added another category to the axiom "All is fair in love and war." Their motto was "All is fair is love, war and politics." They knew they couldn't govern the people if they didn't have control.

XIV

PROPER AUTHORITY

The Town Government is the unit of all town departments. The Selectmen are our town fathers. They are, or
should be, responsible to the people for the overall operation
of government. In a democracy the government must be
responsive to the peoples' will.

Through bits of legislation down through the years the
town departments, both elective and appointive, have been
made somewhat independent of the Selectmen. The Selectmen used to fix the wages of the police, fire and town
employees. That's all gone. They had jurisdiction over the
elective departments. That's all gone. In the subsequent string
of reforms to correct the wrongs of the old political machine,
the pendulum instead of stopping on dead center swung too
far the other way. The power that the Selectmen once had is
gone.

The voting public has no right to expect responsible government from their Selectmen when in most town departments the tail is wagging the dog.

The Old Ring's advisory board was made up of the
department heads. Their theory was, "Who knows more
about the operation of the department than the department
head himself?" They did not think it was common sense, for
example, that the Highway Superintendent should submit his
budget for study and approval to an advisory board made up
of clam diggers, gas station attendants and so forth.

Each year Boss Smith announced a month in advance of
the town meeting, what the tax rate would be. He gave that
figure to his advisory board (the heads of all town departments) and told them to fit their figures into his announced

tax rate, allowing each a 5% cushion against unforeseen expenses. The tax rate was always exactly what Smith said it would be.

The Old Ring controlled the elections and the Town Meeting and with all its faults and it had many, held an iron fist over the department heads and did not allow them to run wild and do as they damn pleased. As bad as they were they gave our town far better government than the kind we have today. That may seem strange. But our country did not grow up on the Declaration of Independence and the Constitution, but rather on big city and small town political machines that were dotted all over this land. They made their own laws.

While none of us want a return to that kind of rule, most historians will agree that the old-time political boss meted out far better government than the kind we have today.

The Old Ring did not have improvement associations barging in on their selectmen's meeting making demands for improvements in their sections and none for the rest of the town.

Once, during my twelve years on the Board of Selectmen, thirty members of the Green Hill Improvement Association stormed into one of our meetings. We looked them over and only two of them were on the voting list. Before the spokesman opened his mouth he was told that whatever their demands were, the answer was, "no." Some confusion followed but that was as far as they were pushing us around.

At the start of 1946, I made a deal with the two other Selectmen. They were both in the express business and were out of town most every day. I asked them to vote me full authority to act for the board in all matters that did not require the action of the full board and, in return, I promised them that I would get a vote through the town meeting that the Selectmen's salaries be as follows: Chairman, $4,000 per year, other members, $1,800 per year. In the town meeting of March 9th, 1946, I made that motion and it passed without a dissenting vote and for one year I was the political boss of the Town of Hull.

All that year I was a full-time Selectman. I was at the Selectmen's Office from 9 a.m. to 5 p.m. every working day and anytime I was out of the office the clerk knew where to find me. I took care of my dentistry in the evenings, Saturdays, Sundays and holidays.

I was in constant contact with the heads of all town departments, working with them and helping them to solve their problems. I was thoroughly convinced that a town as big as ours should be run by a full-time manager and not on the snap judgment of a board meeting for two hours each week.

The state auditors went over the books of the town for that year and when they had finished they sent a letter to the Board of Selectmen congratulating them and stating that the town accounts were in the best condition that they had been in many years.

In the town meeting of March, 1947, the full-time job was thrown out and the Selectmen's salaries were put back to where they were before.

In all government, whether Town, State or National, authority comes from the top down. There must be a leader. The geese in the sky know that.

In my many years on the Board of Selectmen, I tried hard to keep the authority at the top. We fired the Superintendent of Garbage for not doing as he was told. We fired the Chief of the Fire Department for the same reason. We later called the Police Chief's attention to the wrong doings of one of his police officers. We ordered the Chief to transfer him to another section of the town. One of my colleagues on the board suggested that the officer be put out in the ocean in a rowboat without oars. The chief backed up his officer and refused to do as he was told. We tried, by an article in the special town meeting, August 4, 1947, to have the civil service statutes taken away from the Police Chief.

Some felt we should have fired him but he knew and we knew that if the case came before the State Civil Service Commission, even in the slightest disciplinary action, the decision always went against the Selectmen. The Civil Service seemed to think that insubordination in town police departments was perfectly all right. It must be pointed out that at the time of his dismissal the Chief of the Fire Department was not under Civil Service.

There was never any intention on our part to fire the Chief of Police. We simply had no reason to. We wanted to put him in a position so that he would be more responsive to the authority of the Selectmen. What's wrong with that? In a carefully worded speech, I explained to the people of Hull that we were trying to keep the authority in the Board if Selectmen where it rightfully belonged. We were badly beaten in that attempt.

The Old Ring never let the government get out of hand. We tried hard to maintain that virtue. The day of the political boss was gone. A newer generation was rising up before us and I was caught in the big whirlpool caused by the tide that was going out and the one that was coming in.

I thought then and I do today that the governing authority belonged in the Board of Selectmen and not in the hands of any subordinate. When the direction is lost from the top there's trouble ahead.

While we of today take pride in not having the bad habits of the Old Political Ring, we must admit that we don't have some of their good points either. It would be well for us to look back and study the capers of the past, since we cannot learn as much from the few that are living as we can from the many that are dead.

XV

FRIENDS

In March, 1951, running for re-election to the Board of Selectmen, I got a proper pasting. Since experience is the best teacher, here is where we learn lessons that are never taught in the classroom.

When the election results were announced my "friends" all started to walk away from me and like a whipped dog I headed home with my tail between my legs. I opened the door, turned on the light and sat in my favorite seat in the living room. The house was empty.

The rest of my family had gone to a wake. They should have stayed home for mine. Not a living soul came in to place a hand on my shoulder. After sitting there for some time, the telephone rang. I answered it. An old lady called. She gave me her name, that's all that was said. She sobbed her heart out for a few moments and softly placed the receiver back on the hook. Nine months later, one evening a week before Christmas, I sat alone in the same seat in the living room. On a nearby table there were four hundred Christmas Cards in small boxes for my friends. What friends?

I took one stony look at life as it really was, life as I saw it. I opened one box. I took out one card and put the cover back on. I sent out only one card and that to the old lady who called me up so I could hear her cry.

My wife and I recently visited a lady we knew in a nearby rest home. Her husband passed away. Her home was all paid for but she felt lonely living there although she had ten thousand dollars from his life insurance and a modest pension from the Post Office Department. She suggested that her nephew and his wife come live with her. They agreed and moved in. She agreed to deed the home over to them and they in turn agreed that she would have a home as long as she lived. A short time after that, her insurance money gone, she was railroaded off to the rest home. It was about three years after that we visited her. I asked her then how her nephew and his wife were. The poor soul broke down in tears. She said she had not heard a word from them in two years.

The nurse in charge of the rest home was a classmate of mine in High School and so I left my wife with the lady while I talked with the nurse. She had spent most of her life working in rest homes. We talked about this lady's plight and she told me of the amazing number of old people in similar sad straits.

Old folks in the evening of life with the tide going out. We can learn about friends from them. They know that in prosperity our friends know us. In adversity we know our friends.

The big politician addressing his audience starts out by saying, "My friends." He has no friends. All those voting for me across the years were my constituents. My friends were in my living room on the evening that I went down to defeat.

If all you have is loaf of bread and your friend wants it, you break it in half, give him one half and as long you hold on to the other half he is your friend to the death. Give him the other half and he has got all he wanted from you and "Presto" you're looking at an ingrate.

One time I tried to get a man appointed to one of the real good jobs in the town. Neither of the other town Selectmen would go along with me. I pleaded with one so persistently for a year and a half that he finally threw up his hands and the man was appointed. I learned two years later, through the most reliable authority, that his wife wiped herself with one of my Christmas cards. I should have put some holly on the card so she would scratch her ass. That was about all she was capable of.

In politics, gratitude is for favors expected. Never for favors granted.

I imagine we all wonder from time to time, why there are so many mean people in the world and if we had no birth control there would be many more. Perhaps we may find solace in the good behavior of the busy little bee in the following poem:

> The bumblebee is such a busy soul
> That he has no time for birth control
> And that is why in times like these
> We see so many sons of bees.

XVI

FAMOUS PERSONALITIES

Opera Singer

The following article appearing March 13, 1913, in the *New York Evening Mail*, shows the prominence Mme Bernice De Pasquali held in the world of music.

"Mme. Bernice De Pasquali, most famous of American coloratura sopranos, will appear as soloist at the Evening Mail Concert by the Russian Symphony Orchestra in Carnegie Hall Friday evening, is unique in her ability to sing no less than fifty-four operas, one of the most extensive repertories ever possessed by a singer. Nearly every one of these operas the soprano can sing on a few hours notice.

"Of this number, Mme De Pasquali has appeared in fifteen different roles at the Metropolitan Opera House. Familiar to her host of admirers have seen her portrayals in *Lucia, Traviata, Rigoletto, Elisir d'Amore, Don Pasquali, Martha, Pagliacci, Carmen, La Boheme, Nozze di Figaro,* and *Barbier di Siviglia.*

"This bird-voiced singer is a Boston girl, but has spent many years in New York, where she began her early work under Osca Saenger. She is entirely American trained, having never had a single day's tuition abroad.

"Few of the stars of the Metropolitan have ever attained so genuine a success, which dated from her memorable debut in *Traviata* here in 1908.

"Her first operatic appearance was in Milan about seven years ago.

"The amount of melody and the multitudinous sequence

of words in Italian, French and English which Mme De Pasquali carries in mind, is astounding to lay intellects. At a half hour's notice she can appear in costume and sing almost any one of her prodigious repertory.

"When she appeared in The Marriage of Figaro at the Metropolitan for the first time, she had been given eight days to learn the role by Gustav Mahler, then conductor. Despite this disadvantage, the coloratura shouldered the task imposed, faced her audience and scored tremendous success. After the first rehearsal, Conductor Mahler went to her, seized her hand and shook it effusively.

"He congratulated her, 'Madam, you are wonderful,' he cried.

"The perfection of the role, which was a difficult one, had been attained in record time.

"Mme De Pasquali has appeared often with Caruso, Bonci, Scotti, Didur, Amato, Renaud, Gadske, Farrar and other Celebrities and has invariably shared in the highest honors.

"The singer is a woman of plain tastes and she makes study her chief diversion. Her voice never receives less than 6 or 8 hours attention daily. By no means does she sing all this time at full voice. Only her exercises call for the regular exertion necessary for the maintenance of power and flexibility. Much of the time is spent in reviewing or learning words, getting into spirit of the works she studies and memorizing melodies. 'The artist must not stand still,' she often asserts. 'I am absolutely wedded to the old maxim that if one does not progress one goes backwards.'

"Also a first-class pianist, Mme Pasquali likes to spend an hour now and then with old favorite composers, and she exercises her fingers just as though she did not have a voice of stellar importance to be always considered to the exclusion of everything else. But the piano is sheer diversion.

"Friday night she will sing the 'Mad Scene' from Hamlet, by Thomas, accompanied by the Russian Symphony Orchestra

Mme Bernice (James) De Pasquali, world famous opera singer, (1873-1925)
(Courtesy Mary Torre)

under Modest Altschuler, and a group of American songs."
"Mme de Pasquali was honored by being selected as the only
soloist to sing before the Prince of Wales and other dignitaries
at the State concert in commemoration of the founding of
Quebec, in July, 1908, and upon the recent retirement of the
celebrated Madame Sembrich, succeeded that prima donna
in the Metropolitan Opera Company, New York City."*

In her first performance in the Metropolitan Opera House
in 1908, she had to take twenty-six curtain calls.

In February, 1912, in Rigoletto, at the Metropolitan Opera
House she sang the part of Gilda with Enrico Caruso as Il
Duca.

Caruso said at the time, "He was glad to again have the
great pleasure of signing with Mme De Pasquali and that he
had a very exalted opinion of her ability."

On Christmas Eve, 1913, after being introduced by Mayor
Ralph, she sang the principal role of Gilda from a stage erected
at Lotta's Fountain in San Francisco's Newspaper Row, before
100,000 people.

She came back many times on Christmas Eve, to her home
town of Hull, to sing "Silent Night," and other songs of
Christmas in Elm Square in front of the Public Library.

Although, as is the case of most renowned people, many
other localities have tried to claim her as their own, she
belonged to Hull, in every sense of the word. The records of
the town clerk's office show her to be born Bernice James,
30 Main Street, December 7, 1873, Father, William Wallace
James, Mother, Eliza Ann Lucihe both of Hull. Father born
in Boston, occupation Mariner, Mother born in Hull.

Her husband Salvitori DePasquali passed away in 1923.

* Taken from "Joshua James" by Sumner I. Kimball, 1909

In the winter of 1925, at the age of 52, she was laid to rest with her husband in the village cemetery a little more than a stone's throw from where she was born.

The deep affection in which she was held can best be described by those beautiful words written by her mother and inscribed on her tombstone:

"With deepest sorrow we mourn and cry
Until we met again good-by, dear heart good-by."

Lifesaver

Joshua James, greatest lifesaver of all time, is one of the Coast Guard's most neglected heroes. He saved more than a thousand persons from the seas of Hull, Massachusetts, over a sixty-year span–from the age of fifteen until he dropped dead on the beach at the age of seventy-five. He wore the highest lifesaving medals awarded by the United States Government and the Massachusetts Humane Society for the almost incredible heroism, seamanship and resourcefulness he displayed on countless occasions.

William James (no relation), the great American philosopher, wrote letters to Joshua expressing the profound influence of Joshua's feats upon his philosophical thinking: he seemed amazed that the human spirit could soar so high, that one man could and would so persistently and unhesitatingly face extreme peril and under-go such hardships in the service of others. In his own day, Joshua was known and respected throughout the world. Today, only sixty-seven years after death, he is all but forgotten.

Except for his grave, there was nothing to mark his memory even in his own hometown until recently when Hull Selectmen, at the request of the First Coast Guard District and the Hull Historical Society, named a small park in his honor. Our history books, so crowded with names of men

JOSHUA JAMES, WORLD'S GREATEST LIFESAVER,
1826-1902   *(Courtesy First District U.S. Coast Guard)*

who earned lasting fame through one spectacular moment of slaughter on the battlefield, have no space for this man who never killed a single enemy for the glory of his country.

Born in Hull in 1826, Joshua was in the coast-wide shipping trade until he joined the U.S. Lifesaving Service at the age of sixty-two. For the forty-seven years prior to that he was a volunteer member of the Massachusetts Humane Society. In 1886, the Society struck a special silver medal for him, honoring "brave and faithful service of more than 40 years." But the real career of Joshua James had hardly begun.

The most famous rescue of his career, for which he received the Society's Gold Medal, as well as the Gold Lifesaving Medal from the United States Government, was in 1888. He and his men saved the lives of twenty-nine persons from four vessels on November 25 and 26.

The storm of this event was the greatest known in Hull, sweeping the Atlantic coast from the Carolinas to Maine. Early in the morning of the 25th, Captain James and a few of his beachmen climbed to the top of Telegraph Hill for observation, and saw several schooners through the blinding snow. Joshua knew they could not withstand the storm, so he alerted his crews and ordered a beach patrol starting at two in the afternoon. Hardly had it begun when the three-masted Cox and Green was aground broadside on the beach. Nine men were removed by breeches buoy.

The second three-masted schooner, the *Gertrude Abbot,* was found an eighth of a mile farther up the beach just as the first rescue was completed. It was dark and this vessel was too far from shore to use the breeches buoy, and rescue by lifeboat was so dangerous, that Joshua asked for volunteers from his volunteer crew, warning that chances were they would never return from this attempt. All were willing to go with him. People gathered and built a great bonfire on Souther's Hill, assisting the boat's crew. The boat was filled by every wave– and two men were kept busy bailing. They

JOSHUA JAMES AND HIS LIFE SAVING CREW, 1899

(*Courtesy Maurice P. Murphy*)

CHBOSN Kenneth N. Black, officer in charge of Point Allerton Coast Guard Station, decorates the grave of Joshua James, famous past   keeper of the station. Joshua's granddaughter Eva Galiano and grand-nephew Leon Galiano attended the ceremony. August 4, 1967.

GRAVE OF JOSHUA JAMES
Pall Bearers were his lifesaving crew.
(Courtesy Captain Paul B. Cronk U.S.C.G. ret.)

got to the vessel and the eight stranded sailors dropped one by one into their outstretched arms. Getting back to shore was the hardest part. The large crowd on shore watched the desperate struggle, cheering one moment, gasping the next. Two hundred yards from shore the boat struck a boulder and rolled under water– but the crew shifted weight and saved the boat. But a monster wave lifted it high and smashed it on the rocks. All the men managed to reach the hands of the crowd, which had rushed into the surf to assist them. At nine o'clock all were safe ashore. Joshua and his men resumed the patrol.

At three in the morning they found the third three-masted schooner, the *Bertha F. Walker,* aground. They had to go four miles for a boat to replace the one lost. The boat was a new untested one designed by Joshua's brother Samuel. (It was an axiom of the service that the lifesavers might fail in an unfamiliar boat even though it was a better boat. This added greatly to the danger.) However, they rescued the seven survivors without mishap.

While the third rescue was still in progress a messenger on horseback arrived with the news of two more wrecks at Atlantic Hill. The other lifesaving crews were on the scene, and they handled one of the cases. They had tried unsuccessfully on the other– the *H. C. Higginson,* with five men in the rigging. Joshua and his men launched their boat and struggled for forty-five minutes, only to be washed back ashore with two holes stove in the new boat. They patched the boat and tried again, this time reaching the vessel. With difficult maneuvers and great suspense they got the five men into the boat. The body of the steward had all the time been bound to the topmast, and they could not remove it, so it remained overlooking the scene.

Captain James and his men got their first rest in twenty-four hours after this fourth rescue.

The U.S. Lifesaving Service built a station at Stony Beach in 1889, and world famous Joshua was the natural choice for

Keeper. He was sixty-two –seventeen years past the max-imum age limit for original appointments, but this requirement was waived. That year and eleven years later at seventy-three, Joshua passed all physical examinations with no difficulty.

For the record, under past experience qualifying him for the position, Joshua wrote "Fisherman." He took the oath of office October 22, 1889, as Keeper of Point Allerton Station. The following spring he chose seven of his most fearless men as his crew.

An unusual rescue was made on December 16, 1896, when the three-masted schooner *Ulrica* was wrecked in a northeast gale and thick snowstorm three miles south of the Point Allerton Station. Joshua engaged a local farmer and two horses to rush the boat to the scene. The trainmaster of the electric train from Boston, hearing of the emergency, put the train at the service of the lifesaving crew and rushed them to the scene.

The schooner was 500 yards offshore. On the first two tries, the boat was thrown back on the beach. On the third try Joshua was thrown from the boat. The boat passed over him. He came up, grabbed the end of an oar and was dragged back to shore with the boat.

Realizing he could not get the boat out, Joshua took command of the beach apparatus. A line was fired to the ship and secured, but it was too low for a breeches buoy. Joshua and his men got back in the boat and used the rope as a trolley line to pull themselves out to the vessel. The stranded sailors were so numb with cold that one of the lifesavers had to climb aboard and help them off the schooner.

The crowning achievement of Joshua's career was the rescue work in the storm of November, 1898. The storm was even worse than the one in 1888. On the morning of Novem-ber 27, Joshua and his men rescued two survivors of thirteen men in two vessels dashed on Toddy Rocks. Then they took in a family whose home was threatened by the storm. Next,

JOSHUA JAMES FUNERAL, COFFIN IN THE LIFEBOAT
(Courtesy Paul B. Cronk U.S.C.G. ret.)

by breeches buoy, the removed seven men from a three-masted schooner. After that they fought their way to a barge in the surf and rescued five men. All that night they kept a constant patrol.

The second day they rescued three men from a schooner, then three men from Black Rock. For forty-eight hours they were engaged in continuous rescue work. Joshua said of the storm, "We succeeded in getting every man that was alive at the time we started for him, and we started at the earliest moment in each case."

The dramatic death of Joshua James occurred on March 19, 1902. Two days earlier the entire crew, save one of the Monomoy Point Life-saving Station, perished in a rescue operation. This tragedy affected Joshua deeply, and convinced him of the need of even more rigid training of his own crew. So at seven o'clock in the morning of March 19, with a northeast gale blowing, he called his crew for drill. For more than an hour the seventy-five-year-old man maneuvered the boat through the boisterous sea. He was pleased with the boat and with the crew. Upon grounding the boat, Skipper James stepped onto the wet sand and gazed out on the sea. He said, "The tide is ebbing." And on those words he slumped down on the beach and died from sudden failure of his brave old heart.

With his coffin in a lifeboat, Joshua James was carried to his final resting place. Another lifeboat made of flowers was placed on his grave. His tombstone shows the Massachusetts Humane Society seal and bears the inscription "Greater love hath no man than this– that a man lay down his life for his friends."

Both the era of the big sailing ships and the life of Joshua James are closed. But Captain James will always be regarded, by those who go down to the sea in ships, as the Patron Saint of Lifesavers.

XVII

PROPHET WITHOUT HONOR

It's strange indeed, that of these two once famous person-alities, in their time known all over the world, not one in a hundred here in their own home town know anything at all about them and seem to care less.

All this may be seen in the case of Walter Sweeney, of the nearby town of Cohasset. He grew up in this neighborhood. We all knew him and the family. He was an outstanding end on the Syracuse University football team and went on from there to the San Diego Chargers of the American Football League.

He was chosen year after year on the All Star team and is regarded by most of the experts as one of the greatest guards in professional football.

There have been many pictures and stories in all the Metropolitan Newspapers of Sweeney's exploits on the football field. There was a very nice picture and story a short while back in the *Quincy Patriot Ledger*. But I have never seen his picture or his name in any of the local newspapers of his neighborhood.

He could get his picture and his name in the local papers over and over again if he got drunk and smashed his car into a telephone pole.

A surprising number of men while being elected President of the United States failed to carry their home town.

It seems in a small town that the higher one soars the smaller he looks to those who cannot fly.

The answer must be back, where all answers are, in Holy Scripture. From the New Testament St. Matthew, Chapter

13, verse 57: "A prophet is not without honour, save in his own country, and in his own house."

XVIII

PROHIBITION

After ratification by all the states, except Connecticut and Rhode Island, the Eighteenth Amendment to the Constitution barring the sale and distribution of intoxicating liquor in the United States became effective on January 16, 1920.

Up to that time Nantasket was the only liquor licensed community in southeastern Massachusetts for 125 miles from Boston to the tip of Cape Cod. The town officials and the liquor dealers both licensed and unlicensed went right along as if the Eighteenth Amendment had never existed. The only difference was that the license fees were no longer paid into the town treasury and "Speakeasies" were cropping up all over the place.

Prohibition was a bizarre period throughout the country and Nantasket was no exception. An endearing friendship was maintained between the Coast Guard patrols and the rumrunners plying between the big ships outside the twelve mile limit and the shore. On shore a fist-full of money would always turn a policeman's head the other way.

The rumrunners were more afraid of the Federal Agents than they were of anybody else. When I was a boy my father used to tell me a "tongue in cheek" story of a bandit in Ireland who had the blacksmith put his horse's shoes on backwards so that his pursuers instead of looking for him in the place where he was going would try to find him in the place he had left. A local rumrunner had his boat painted green on one side and red on the other. The Federal Agents would be hiding behind a summer cottage and spot a green boat going out and watch for it to come back and when the red boat came in sight they would pay no attention to it. It was the green boat they were after. This trick didn't always work but it was very confusing to the Federal Agents.

Some of the bigger operators brought the liquor ashore in hydro-planes and a Boston group used a submarine.

Most of the rumrunners used lobster boats and when they would bring their cargo in, usually in five-gallon tins of alcohol, they would fool around, pretend to be tending their lobster raps and slip in when the "coast was clear."

It was amusing to know of some of the local delivery methods. One bootlegger had his small child sitting in a baby carriage and his ten-year-old daughter pushing. Everyday the carriage was pushed down to the cigar counter of the Nantasket Hotel. The man would come out from behind the counter, lift the baby up and remove the booze delivery that the baby was sitting on, put the baby back and send the children on their way.

A "grocery man" would deliver a crate of eggs to a Speakeasy. The top layer would be eggs and the rest of the crate would be filled with booze.

Our town is a peninsula. All the activity is near the entrance. There is only one local cemetery located at the other end of the town. Of the many funeral processions creeping into the town, only about one in every five ever reached the cemetery. The other four would swing in behind some hotel and deliver a shipment of booze.

The ladies of the time had a big advantage over the girls of today. Their skirts were down to the ground. They could make a liquor delivery that the girls of the mini skirt could not.

During the prohibition period all the retail liquor places were known as "Speakeasies." The difficulty the operators ran into was how to advertise their business places. The newspapers couldn't take their ads. A "Speakeasy" operator would get a friend to squeal on him to the Federal Agents so he could get his place raided. The next morning after the raid, the name, address, complete description of the premises and the booze confiscated would be plastered all over the daily papers and he would be on his way to a howling success.

The "Spit-toon" was a well known "Speakeasy." They featured a special drink called Tear Ass Whiskey. It was a powerful beverage. After inhaling a few glasses of Tear Ass when the customer would fart he'd burn a hole in the ass of his pants and the second fart would burn right through the chair. Nobody ever died from drinking Tear Ass but some of us came damn near it.

It was amusing to sit in the place and watch customers step up to the bar and hear the bartender ask, "What are you going to have boys?" One would say, "I think I'll have a Tear Ass and ginger, another would say make mine Tear Ass with a water chaser, a third would say I'll have the same." Tear Ass whiskey was a popular drink in spite of the fact that the fire department kept a close watch and regarded the place as a serious fire hazard.

Another Speakeasy was the Gallstone Café. The place pretended to be a restaurant but no one ever saw any food there. There was no sign on front of the place. The police officer on the beat, who used to drop in occasionally for a "pick-me-up," told the proprietor that he had to pass the place eighteen or twenty times a day and it would look better if he would tack up some kind of food sign. The proprietor agreed. The next day he climbed up on the step ladder and nailed a sign on the front of the building – "Hot Dogs." As he came down, a man with two boys standing at the foot of the ladder ordered three hot dogs. He said, "My good man if I had any, I'd eat them myself."

The Gallstone dealt entirely in Bathtub gin. The customers walked in off the sidewalk through a large empty room into the back kitchen, the bar was the top of an iron cooking stove. There was a sign on the wall back of the stove. It read,

"The MaCoy 40 cents, the Crap 25 cents." Almost everyone ordered the MaCoy until it was found out that both brands came from the same bathtub batch. Then most everyone ordered the Crap. He then took down the old sign and put up another, "Gin 35 cents." He no longer had to ask his patrons "what do you want, the Crap or the MaCoy?"

One barroom that was licensed before prohibition put a sign out over the sidewalk "Drugs." You couldn't buy a dose of salts in the place. The proprietor wielded some political influence. He was head of the Dry Heavers–those who got so sick from the booze that, when they tried to vomit, nothing would come up.

A local friend of mine secured a State license to manufacture hair tonic. He never made a drop of hair tonic. He was alloted quite a quantity of pure alcohol. He sold it to the bootleggers at a handsome profit.

If any place had more than one bathroom it was not a real Speakeasy. In those days ladies did not patronize the Speakeasy. So the men's room was all the facilities that were needed. Sometimes a customer would spend much more time in the men's room than what he went in there for, in order to peruse and scrutinize the literary gems both poetry and prose that adorned the walls. Sometimes a man would stay there so long that a friend would go in to see if he fell through the hold.

On the wall of one Speakeasy men's room this regulation was written. "All turds over a foot long must be lowered with a rope."

This was one of the milder verses. We may as well stop here and keep this book clean so that folks won't have to hide it till the children go to bed.

The skills shown by some of the writers would have carried them far in the literary field but their subject matter would never let them get out of the men's room.

XIX

FAMOUS FIRSTS

First Night Baseball Game

The following is the story of the first night baseball game ever played under the lights in the United States, and for that matter in the World, here at Nantasket Beach in September, 1880.

The Nantasket Beach experiment got more attention in the press. Lee Allen describes it in his *Stove League* (A.S. Barnes & Co.). This was in 1880, mind you, only one year after Thomas Edison invented the electric light bulb. No time wasted there.

"A novel exhibition of electric light was made at Strawberry Hill, Nantasket, last evening," said the story. "What especially attracted the 300 spectators to the balconies of the Sea Foam House was the promise of a baseball game played after dark.

"The real significance of the occasion, however, was the first public experiment in illustration of a new system of illuminating towns by electricity. It contemplates an innovation of startling magnitude.

"The apparatus in use consisted of 36 carbon lamps in the communication with a dynamoelectric generator that is operated by an engine of 30 horsepower. To support the lamps three wooden towers were erected, 100 feet high and 500 feet apart, so as to overlook a triangular spot just beneath the northern piazza of the Sea Foam House.

"The lamps were disposed 12 in a group and possessed a total lighting power of 90,000 candles or 30,000 for each tower. An idea of the effect produced by the illumination may be best conceived by stating the fact that a flood of mellow light thrown upon the field enabled the ball players, between 8:00 and 9:30, to complete a game of nine innings.

"The nines were picked from the employees of Jordan Marsh & Co. and R.H. White & Co. and tied the game with a score of 16 to 16.

"It cannot be said the practice of such sports is likely to be carried out extensively by night rather than by day, for the players had to bat and throw with some caution, and the number of errors due to imperfect light was high.

"Boston did the experimenting. It's too bad it didn't have the honor of playing the first Major League night game."

Verification of this fact can be found, in any of the large libraries and book stores, on page 499, *The Official Encyclopedia of Baseball*, Revised Edition, 1956.

First Lighthouse

Boston Light is America's oldest lighthouse, established on Little Brewster Island in the town of Hull, September 14, 1716. Its maintenance was paid for by a tax of a penny per ton on all vessels except coasters moving in or out of Boston Harbor.

The first keeper, George Worthylake, with annual salary of fifty pounds, also acted as harbor pilot. In 1718 he, his wife and daughter were drowned when the lighthouse boat capsized as they were returning from Boston to the Island. Benjamin Franklin, then a young printer, wrote a ballad about the incident, "Lighthouse Tragedy," and sold it on the streets of Boston.

During the Revolutionary War, the British captured little Brewster Island, and when forced to evacuate in 1776, blew up the lighthouse. The new lighthouse, which is the one still in service, was built in 1783 for fourteen hundred and fifty

BOSTON LIGHT
Boston Light House in preparation for Christmas visit of Flying Santa
Claus, Edward Rowe Snow, noted marine historian, 1966.
(Courtesy CHBOSN Kenneth N. Black, U. S. Coast Guard)

pounds supplied by the Massachusetts Legislature. In 1790 it was ceded to the Federal Government.

In 1813, keeper Jonathan Bruce and his wife witnessed the famous battle between the American Chesapeake and the British Shannon in which the mortally wounded Captain Lawrence uttered his immortal words, "Don't give up the ship."

When Captain Tobias Cook of Cohasset was keeper in 1844, a Spanish cigar factory was set up on the island, with young girls from Boston brought to work in it, in an effort to deceive Boston smokers that cigars manufactured there were imported. The business was soon exposed as a fraud and discontinued.

In 1856, the height of the tower was raised to 98 feet.

On November 2, 1861, the square rigger *Maritana* ran into heavy seas in Massachusetts Bay and approached Boston in a blinding snow, driven by a howling southeaster. At one o'clock in the morning of November 3, she sighted Boston Light and headed for it, but crashed on Shag Rocks, soon after, with passengers and crew ordered into the weather chains after the crew had cut the masts away. The shi broke in two and the captain was crushed to death, but seven persons floated to Shag Rocks atop the pilot house, while five others swam to the ledge, as fragments of the wreckage started coming ashore on both sides of Little Brewster Island. A dory from the pilot boat rescued the survivors from the rocks.

When the *Fanny Pike* went ashore on Shag Rocks in 1882, Keeper Thomas Bates rowed out and took the crew safely off the ledge.

In 1893 the Massachusetts Institute of Technology sent twenty or thirty students to live on the island, while experiments were made with various types of foghorns in an endeavor to find one that would penetrate the area known as the "Ghost Walk" six or seven miles to the east.

On Christmas Day, 1909, the five-masted schooner *Davis Palmer,* heavily loaded with coal, hit Finn's Ledge and went down with all hands.

When the USS Alacrity was wrecked on the ice-covered ledges off the island on February 3, 1918, Keeper Jennings and his assistants made four attempts to shoot a rope to the doomed ship but each time the rope parted. Jennings then brought the lighthouse dory to the shore, and assisted by two naval reservists, pushed it over the ice and into the surf. Twenty-four men were clinging to the wreck in perilous positions when he reached it after a dangerous trip. Flinging a line aboard, they began the rescue of the half-frozen sailors, four times running the gauntlet of ice rocks and surf until all twenty-four men were saved.

During World War II, the light was extinguished as a security measure, but was again placed in operation July 2, 1945.

The Light is a two million candlepower second-order electric light, flashing white every ten seconds, and visible for sixteen miles. A horn-diaphragm fog signal gives two blasts every sixty seconds during fog. Three enlisted Coast Guardsmen now man the station.

Boston Light is the centerpiece on the seal of the Town of Hull.

First Motorized Pump

The Town of Hull had the first motorized pumping engine in New England. It carried a 500 gallon Rumsey pump built by the Webb Motor Company at Vincennes, Indiana, and was delivered to the Hull Fire Department in 1908.

First Third Rail

In 1896, the first use of the third rail by a surface railroad in the United States was on the Nantasket Beach Railroad's extention to East Weymouth and Braintree.

First Vessel to Pass Through Canal

When the Cape Cod Canal was opened to commercial traffic on July 29, 1914, the first vessel to pass through the canal was the Nantasket Beach paddle-wheeler *Rose Standish*. The private train that brought August Belmont and other dignitaries to the opening was standing on the shore line. Belmont was the New York financier who built the canal.

Odd Items

It is part of folklore that Hull was at one time settled by pirates. While I was on the Board of Selectmen I was accused of carrying on that tradition.

I've told you quite frankly about the bad things I've done. It may be better for all to forget about the good ones.

Instead I'll tell you one of the many nice things the Old Ring did for the town and its people.

In 1919, when the boys had come back from service in World War One, the Old Ring made preparations for a fitting homecoming. Through the Congressman they obtained from the Treasury in Washington a number of blank twenty dollar gold pieces. On one side they had engraved the seal of the Town of Hull, the centerpiece of which is a replica of the

S. S. ROSE STANDISH

S. S. Rose Standish of the Nantasket Line, Captain Osceola James, was the lead vessel in a parade of ships at the ceremonies opening the Cape Cod Canal to commercial traffic, July 29, 1914. The private train that brought August Belmont and other dignitaries was standing on the opposite shore obscured by the boat. Belmont, the New York financier who built the canal was standing in the pilot house when this picture was taken. (*Courtesy R. Loren Graham*)

Boston Lighthouse and a diamond set where the light comes on. On the other side was the inscription:

Presented
to
Veterans Name
by the
Town of Hull
for
World War Service
June 25, 1919

The medal was suspended from a black silk ribbon.

The banquet on the evening of June 25, 1919, in Schlitz famous Palm Garden of the old Paragon Park was attended by Governor Calvin Coolidge, Lieutenant Governor Channing Cox and about every dignitary of any importance in Massachusetts. Half the people of Hull jammed their way into the place; they were literally hanging on the rafters. The menu for that banquet had six different dinners to choose from with champagne and all other drinks.

After the dinner, Governor Coolidge, who later became President of the United States, was introduced by the chairman of the Hull Board of Selectmen, Clarence Nickerson. He was his usual self. He stood up and read the names on the boxes as each veteran walked up to get his medal and he then sat down.

John F. "Honey Fitz" Fitzgerald, whose grandson, John Fitzgerald Kennedy, was later to become President, stood up on a table and sang his old favorite, "Sweet Adeline," as only he could sing it.

That was a memorable occasion that we never forgot.

I have that medal now and I've always cherished it. Thanks to the dear old political machine, we veterans of World War I knew that we belonged to the Town of Hull.

When I was on the Board of Selectmen, I proposed on two separate occasions to have a comparable medal struck off for each of the veterans of World War II, but each time I got no response.

A glance over the shoulder at the past won't do us any harm.

Local Character

Most every small town had its local character. Nantasket was no exception. At the town elections this fellow would cast a write-in vote for himself and when the results were announced the Town Clerk would call out his name and one vote. This went on year after year with the same one vote. He joined the Catholic Church and in the following election he still got the one vote. He then turned Protestant because the priest didn't vote for him.

He was standing in front of the Post Office one day when a summer resident said to him, "I suppose there are quite a few queer people around here." He said, "Yes, but most of them have gone home by Labor Day."

There was a big hearing in the auditorium of the State House about building a bridge from Boston to Nantasket. A city slicker, running true to form questioned the intelligence of the people in the small town. This character jumped up and hollered at him, "I want you to know that the people of Hull is intelligent."

The character was standing with a group of us at the pistol range in the basement of police headquarters. A shooting instructor from the State Police was trying to teach the Hull Police how to shoot. He started them shooting about thirty feet from the target. They all missed it completely. He brought them ten feet closer. Their aim was worse. He moved them almost on top of the target. They all missed it and the instructor threw up his hands in disgust, turned to the local character and said, "Can you teach these men how to shoot a pistol?" He said, "No, but I might be able to show them how to hit a bull in the ass with a snow shovel."

One Sunday afternoon in July, 1896, John L. Sullivan, who had lost his heavyweight crown to Jim Corbett, was having a drink at a table at Pogie's Saloon. A stranger standing at the bar made an insulting remark to him. Sullivan jumped up from his chair. The man flew through the open door so fast that you could play pool on his coattails. As he was going out he grabbed the knob and slammed the door. John L. started an overhand swing right from the floor. His arm crashed through the door and broken pieces of wood and his fist hit the poor fellow in the back of the neck and knocked him cold on the veranda.

A new door was put on the outside of the casing. The shattered door was tied back against the wall, permanently, and a brass plate affixed describing the incident in memory of John L. Sullivan and as a warning to others to keep out of the way of his overhand right punch, especially when it was brought up from the floor.

In the summer of 1908, the State Police got wind that gambling was going on at the two inns on Peddocks Island. They raided the place and arrested one proprietor but couldn't find the other. After they rowed the prisoner back to the mainland he told that his name was John Irwin, Chief of Police of Peddocks Island. After a consultation, in the barroom of the Pemberton Hotel, his innocence was established and they let him go. In the 1908 Town Book, Irwin was appointed by the Selectmen a special policeman without pay for Peddocks Island. The "chief" business was his own invention.

Excerpt from report of Chief of Police for the same year, "...it hardly seems the proper thing for a Town advanced as we are to be obliged to use an open express wagon to convey a man or woman who has been injured to the boat or train, in order to send them to the hospital. One case the past summer we waited forty-five minutes to get an express wagon to move a man who was dying of injuries.

Frank M. Reynolds
Chief of Police"

We were unique in other ways. Before the turn of the century we had a Chairman of the Board of Selectmen for many years who was not a citizen of the United States.

We had a United States Postmaster at Nantasket Beach Post Office who was not a citizen of the United States.

I made a provision in my will that a granite toilet seat be erected on my grave for the convenience of my political enemies. After three months of domestic warfare that provision was finally stricken out.

Fifty Years Later

"Therefore all things whatsoever ye would that men should do to you, do ye even so to them; For this is the law and the prophets."

That's the Golden Rule from the New Testament, Matthew, Chapter 7, Verse 12.

That's the Golden Rule that was practiced by the Pilgrim Fathers and their descendants.

That was the Golden Rule that was lived up to in the American countryside when I was a boy. No family in our neighborhood ever locked the door of their home. If a light was burning in an upstairs window of a home late at night, folks would come over to see if anything was wrong.

I remember one evening, my mother got very sick and we went for our family doctor. He came by horse and buggy from six miles away. He examined my mother with light from a kerosene lamp and asked my father to put his horse in our barn. With the coffee pot on the kitchen stove, that old doctor stayed all night long and did not leave until he felt my mother was well enough for him to go.

We were one of two Irish Catholic families in the neighborhood and at daylight, after the doctor had gone, the Protestant Minister came in and asked if there was anything he could do.

People were honestly concerned about each others welfare. The mark of a good citizen was that he was anxious to help his neighbor.

If a man was putting up or taking down his storm windows a neighbor, passing by, would stop to give him a hand.

I remember, when a coal barge was smashed against the rocks in a winter storm, our next-door-neighbor loaned my father his horse and wagon so that he could go down and pick up some of the coal that was strewn along the beach.

Up to the advent of prohibition our country was a law-abiding people.

The real damage of the prohibition experiment was not the impact on our economy– that could be made-up. The real damage came when seventy percent of the people of the United States stepped outside the law. It made no difference whether a man was drinking bathtub gin in Peoria, Illinois or Tear Ass whiskey at Nantasket Beach, both consumer and purveyor were breaking the law. Without the one the other couldn't be.

Our country is not a geographic area, not the skyscrapers and giant industries, not the might of its armed forces. Our country is the two hundred million Americans who make it up; where our country is going is where they're going because they are the country.

If there is a single factor that more than anything else was responsible for the solid growth of our country from the landing of the Pilgrims to the 18th Amendment of 1920, it's got to be the rigid adherence of the American people to the principles of the Golden Rule.

If the Golden Rule is a symbol of strength, and who can say it's not, then its absence must be a symbol of weakness.

Our people are not inclined to help one another anymore. There's an alarming proportion of Americans who want everything for themselves and will yield nothing to their country or their fellow man. Everyone seems hostile to everyone else.

The child in the public school is barred by the Supreme Court of the United States from asking God to "forgive us our trespasses as we forgive those who trespass against us."

The spectacle of the local doctor who refuses to leave his home to administer to his dying neighbor is a new wrinkle in our society.

The Golden Rule is gone and with it the national fabric that it wove.

Filthy literature on the newsstands of our country was unheard of fifty years ago.

The narcotic peddler of fifty years ago, as bad as he was, never lowered himself to peddle dope to the school children of our country.

It's something new to read of college professors telling the public that the use of narcotics by the children in our schools is perfectly all right. One of them was quoted as saying he had no objection to his eighteen-year-old daughter taking dope.

Today, if you want to find out how to spell marijuana, don't go to the dictionary in the book case, just pick up the nearest newspaper. That's what I did.

Throwing stones and bottles through windows of government buildings– a massive attempt to take over the Pentagon Building in Washington, a mob taking over a Selective Service Office and occupying it all day long, another group trying to tip over a bus that was taking draftees to the induction center, show us that peaceful demonstration is a new term for anarchy.

Draft Director Lewis B. Hershey, on November 8, 1967, sent a letter to all draft boards calling for revocation of draft exemptions for students who interfere with recruiting or Selective Service business or who engage in illegal antiwar protests.

In the week beginning December 4, 1967, Lloyd H. Elliott, President of George Washington University, announced he had "suspended all recruiting by all military services on the campus until General Hershey's letter of November 8, 1967 has been rescinded, overruled or clarified."

Those are examples of our new standard of patriotism.

Crime is getting out of control over the land.

That our country is being eaten away from within there can be no doubt.

No earthly power seems able to stop it. Our only out is God. What can we expect from Him when, with His outstretched hands to help us. we turn and walk away?

Arnold Toynbee, noted British historian, wrote *Civilization on Trial* and many other books. His outstanding work, *A Study of History* (6 vols., 1934-1939), is a monumental analysis of the rise and fall of civilizations and in it we find that of twenty-one known civilizations, nineteen have been destroyed from within.

With those precedents to look back on we have a clearer view of the pattern of history. We know what's coming.

The generations ahead may have to stand on the sidelines and watch and see if the United States of America can do what no other dynasty in all of human history has ever been able to do– stand up when it's rotten from within.

And learn, although too late, what the Pilgrim meant when he stood with one hand raised to God and the other extended to his fellow man.

INDEX

Yes! Please send me my own copy
of "Old Nantasket!"

Name_____

Street Address _____

_____

City_____ State _____ ZIP_____

Telephone: _____

E-mail: _____

No. of Copies	_____
@ **$19.99** each	
Total	$ _____
MA residents add $.99 tax per copy	_____
Shipping $3.00 per copy	_____
Total due	$ _____

Send order to:
Fort Revere Park &
Preservation Society
PO Box 963
Hull, MA 02045-0963

— —

Yes! Please send me my own copy
of "Old Nantasket!"

Name_____

Street Address _____

_____

City_____ State _____ ZIP_____

Telephone: _____

E-mail: _____

No. of Copies	_____
@ **$19.99** each	
Total	$ _____
MA residents add $.99 tax per copy	_____
Shipping $3.00 per copy	_____
Total due	$ _____

Send order to:
Fort Revere Park &
Preservation Society
PO Box 963
Hull, MA 02045-0963